The Official

MANGA & COMICS COLORING BOOK

The Artists and Creators at Saturday AM

ROCKPORT

HOME OF THE WORLD'S MOST DIVERSE MANGA HEROES

Welcome Saturday Playmates!

Whether you are a new Saturday AM fan or one of our long-time supporters, you now hold in your hands something we worked on for many years. To say that we're incredibly proud of this would be a serious understatement. Furthermore, we're even more ecstatic at the chance to try something different with the coloring book model. What's different about the *Official Saturday AM Comics and Manga Coloring Book,* you ask?

Well, let's start with the Saturday AM part! The world's biggest brand for diverse manga series brings their roster of original and exclusive heroes to this book, with awesome scenes and character portraits from hit series like APPLE BLACK and CLOCK STRIKER! Likewise, our popular artists, like Nigerian YouTuber Whyt Manga and American comics pro JeyOdin, are here as well for their first official coloring book project.

Secondly, we provide information on each of the series in full color so you can learn more about the characters as well as see their actual color palettes.

Finally, we've arranged the coloring pages so you can easily take pics and share your work on popular social media platforms like Instagram. After all, we want you to explore your own creativity and show the world how you can provide definition to our characters with unique shading and coloring techniques.

And don't forget to test your art skills even further with the included INKING test pages from Saturday AM's top artists! Finish the artwork in your style and THEN COLOR it for a truly unique showcase of your talents!

And we DO HOPE you'll share your works online with the hashtag #COLORINGSATURDAYAM, as we want to see your works and SHARE THE BEST!

And who knows? Works we really think are amazing may score folks a free manga book, a subscription to our app, or even a contract for future work!

So what are you waiting for?

START COLORING!!

Frederick L. Jones, Publisher, Saturday AM

P.S. Use the QR code to access digital versions of coloring art from this book that you can print out and color by hand or with your preferred software program.

MEET THE HEROES

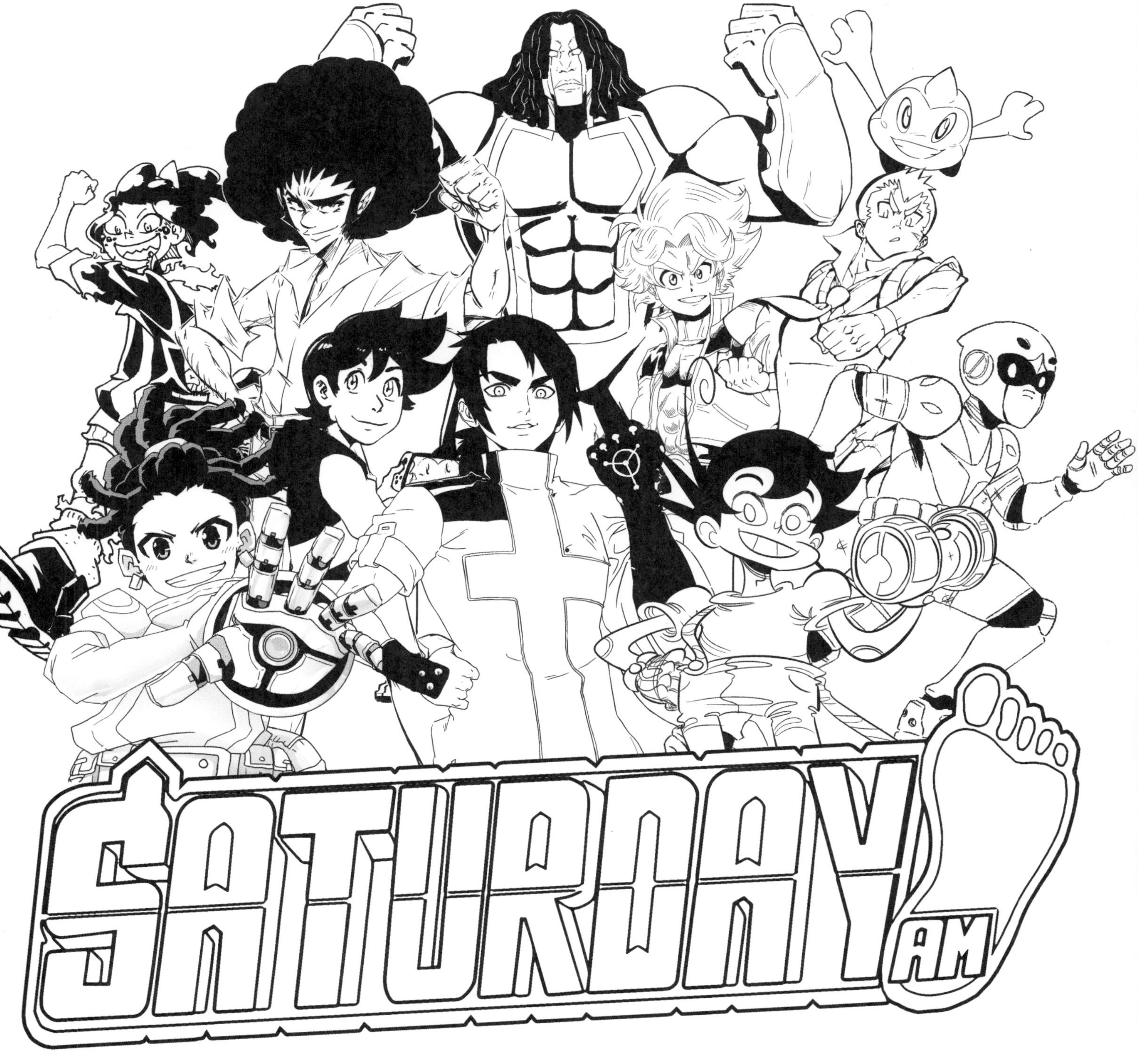
SATURDAY AM

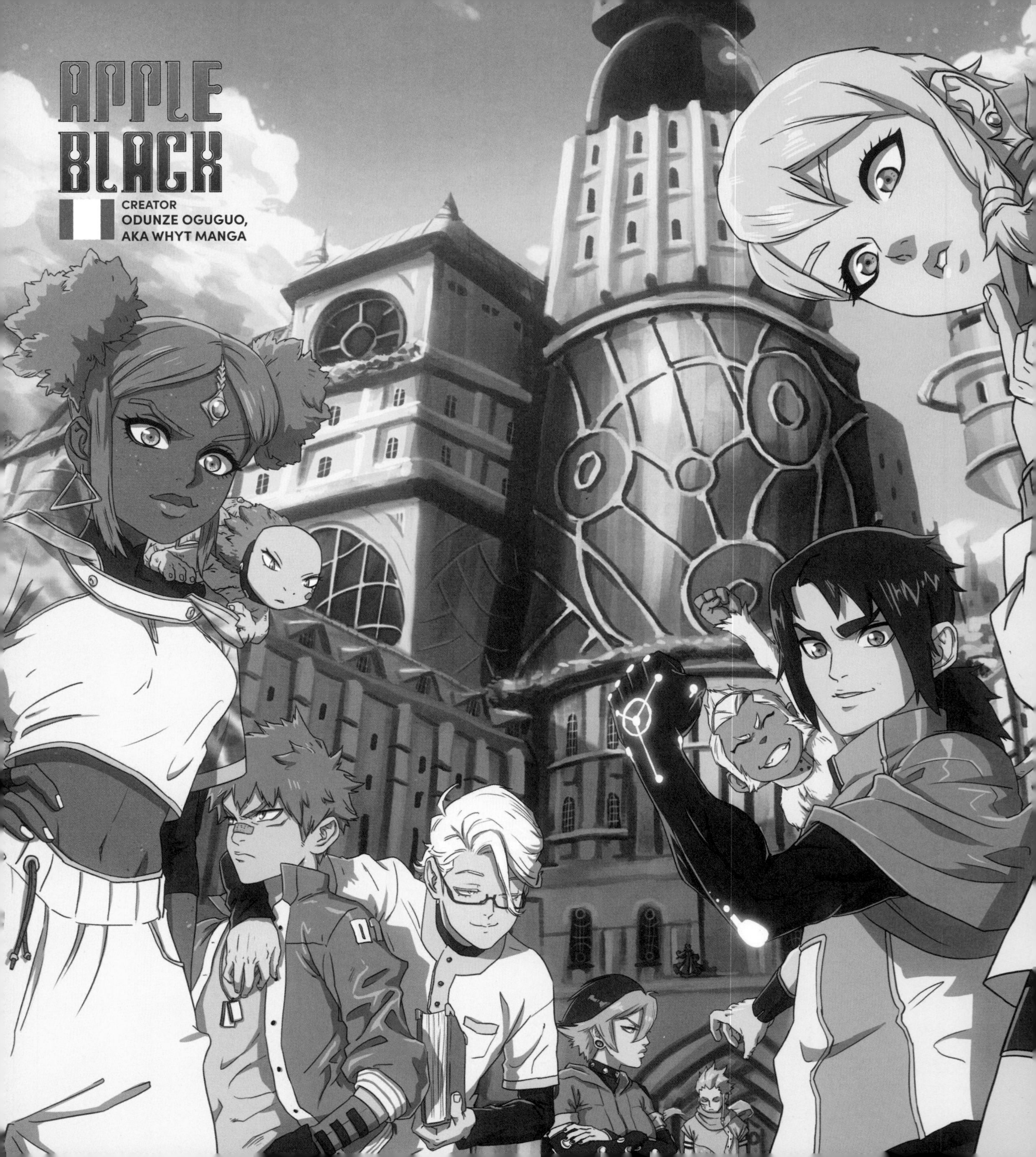
APPLE
BLACK
CREATOR
ODUNZE OGUGUO,
AKA WHYT MANGA

SANO

NAME: SANO BENGOTE TAMASHII

HEIGHT: 5'6"

SERIES: APPLE BLACK

BIO: Sano is brave, kind, perceptive, and socially awkward. He can teleport while possessing unforeseen power with his sentient god-like arm, Arodihs. Sano primarily uses Arodihs to form energy-based attacks and defenses.

APPLE
BLACK

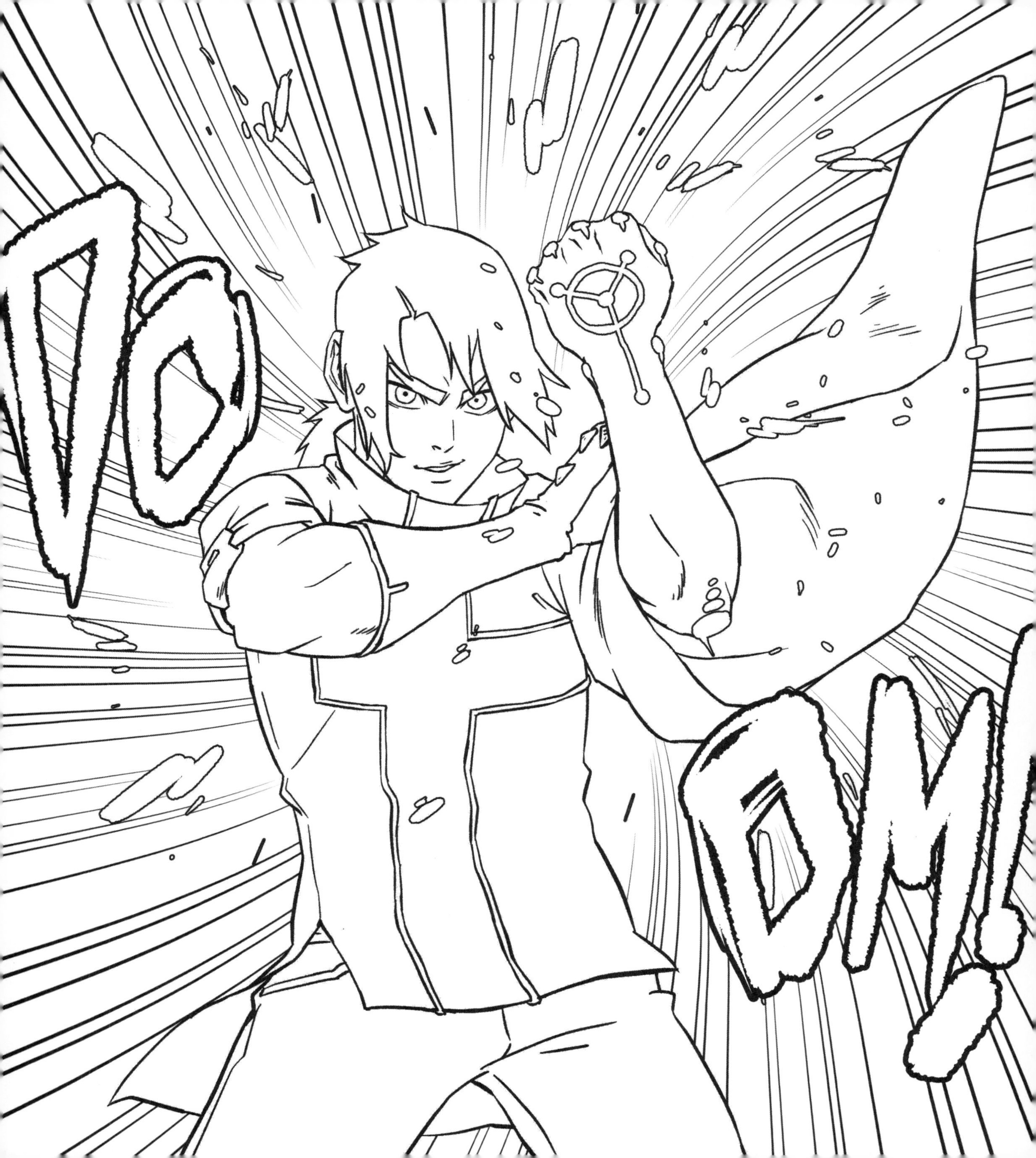
DOOM!

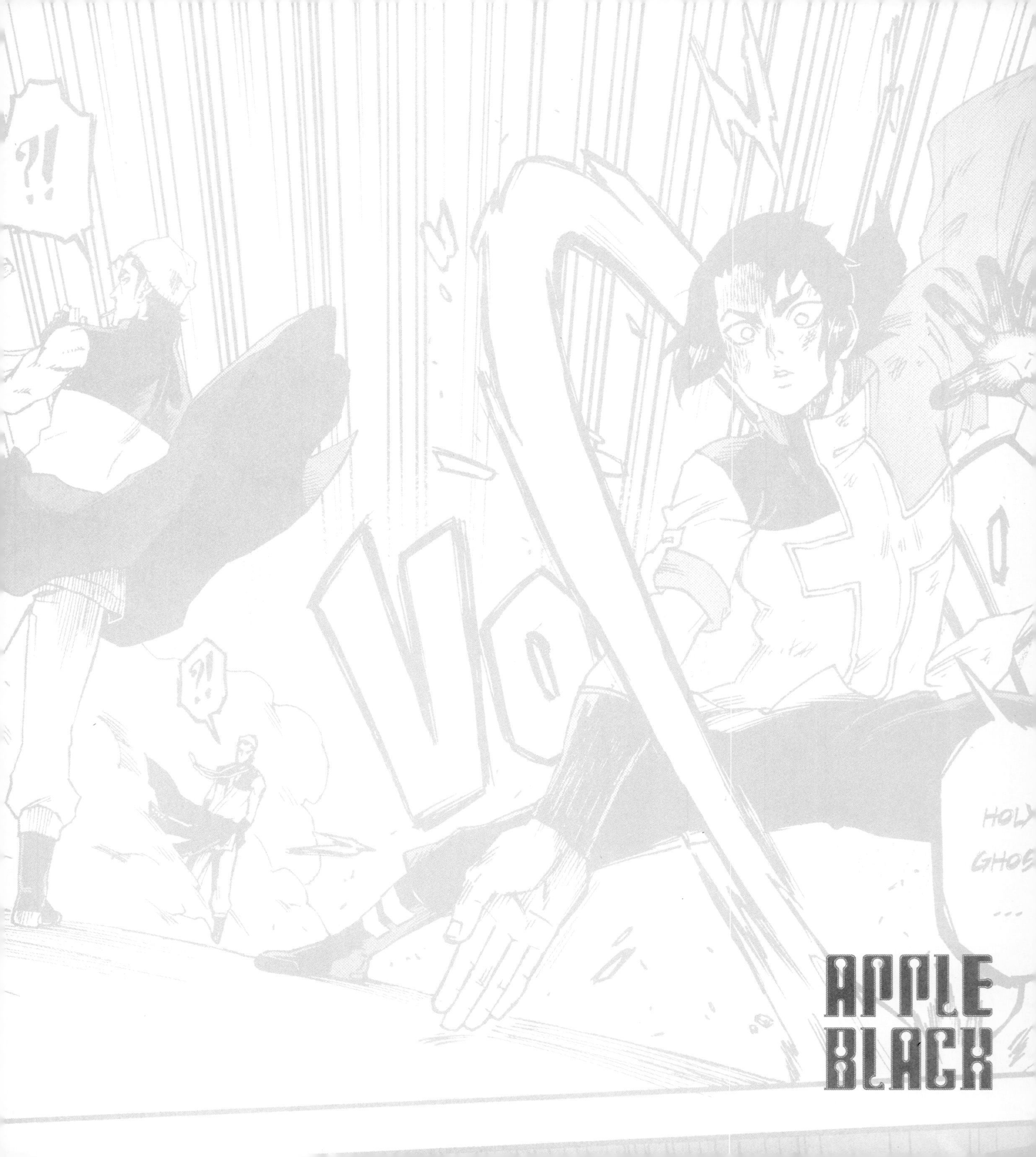

?!
?!
VO
HOLY
GHOS
...
APPLE
BLACK

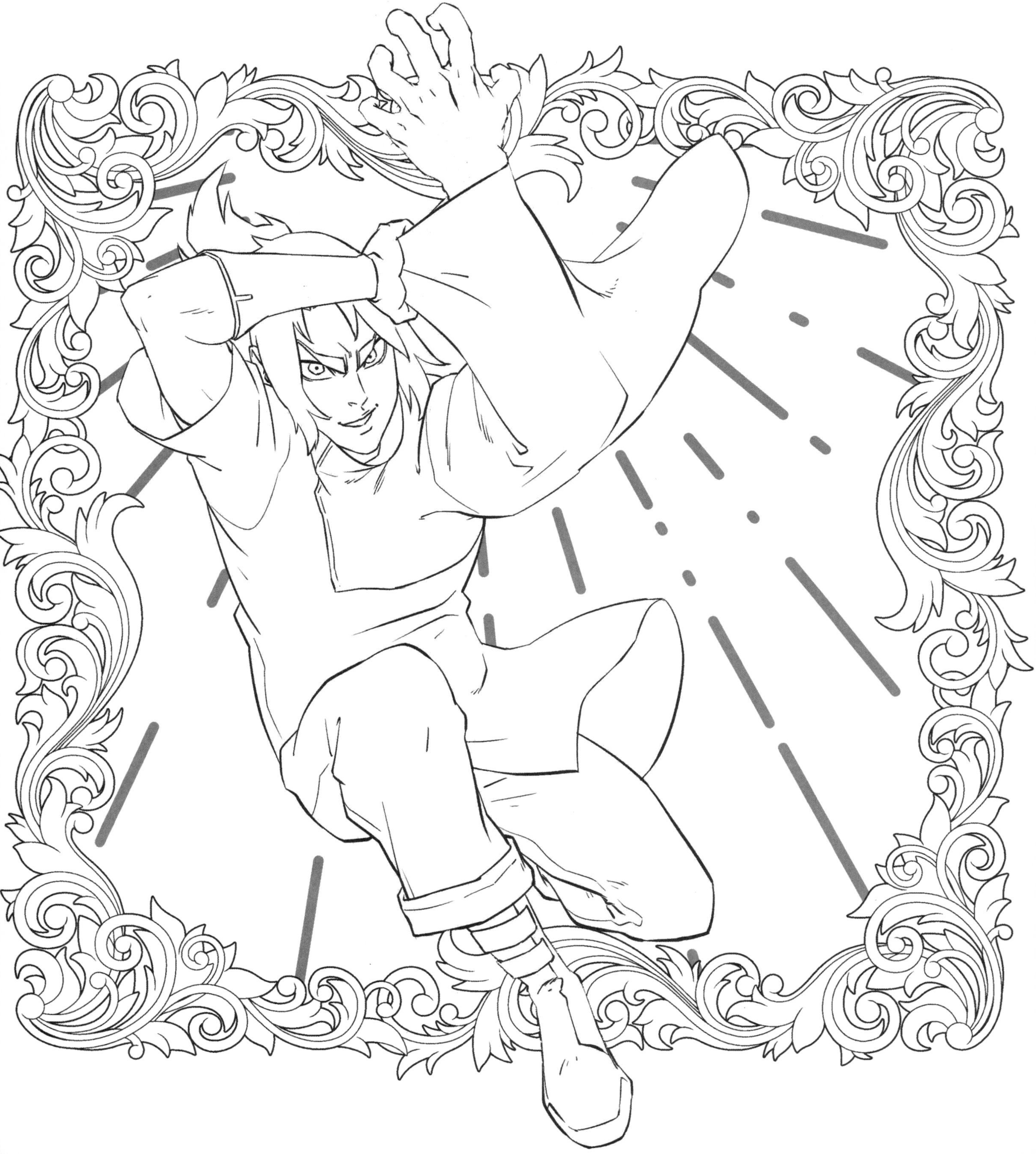

APPLE BLACK

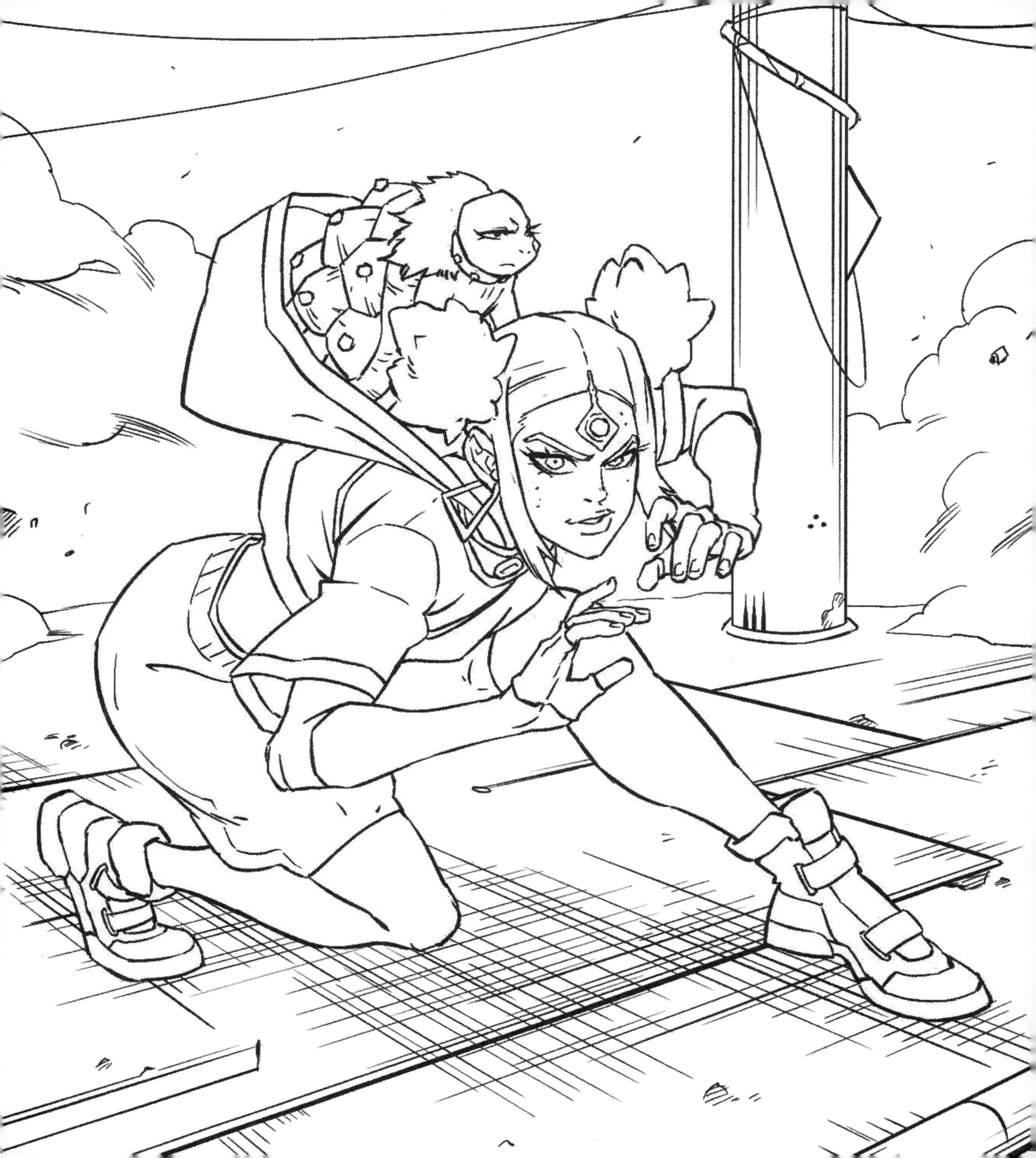

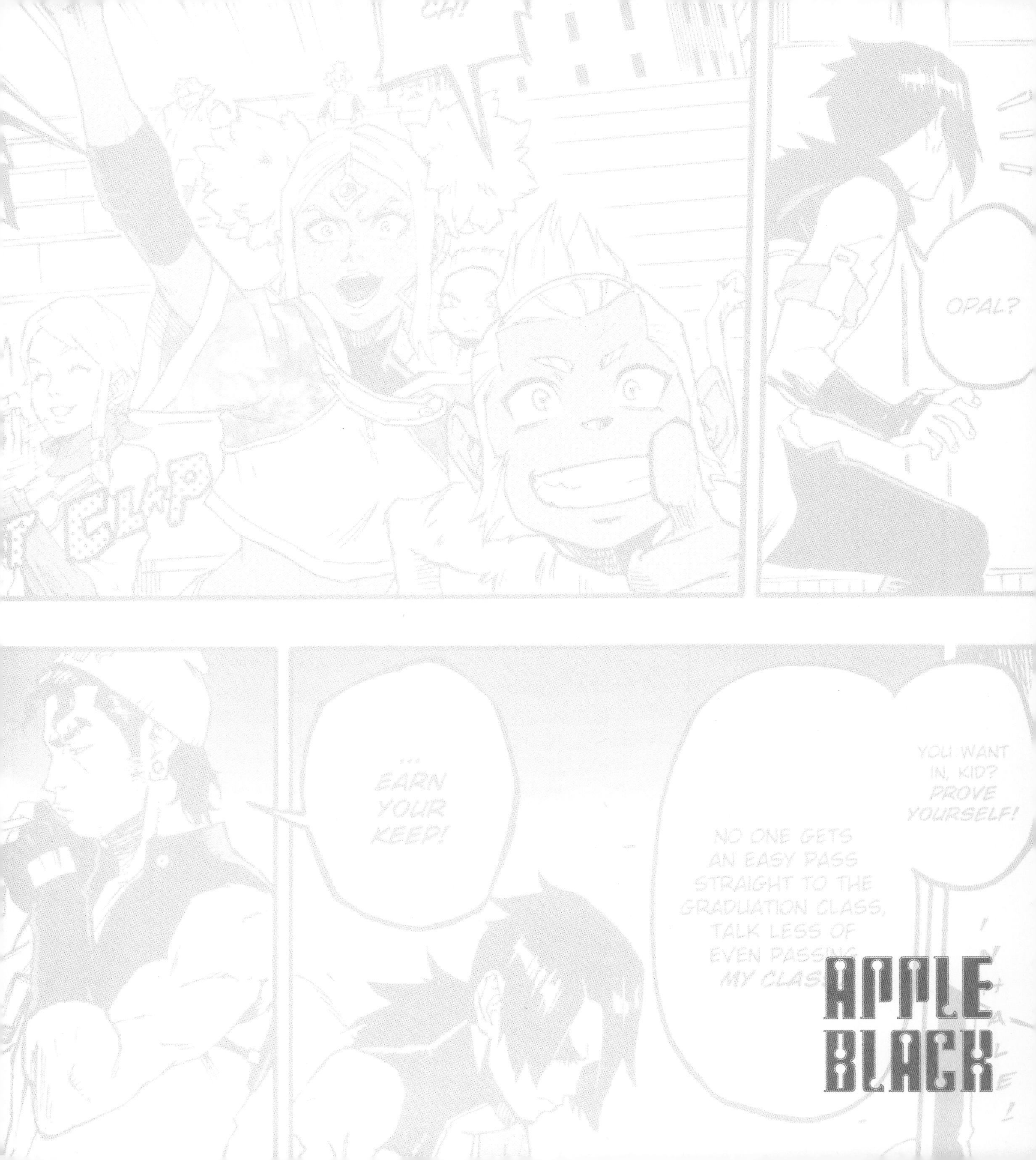

CH!
CLAP
OPAL?
...EARN YOUR KEEP!
YOU WANT IN, KID? PROVE YOURSELF!
NO ONE GETS AN EASY PASS STRAIGHT TO THE GRADUATION CLASS, TALK LESS OF EVEN PASSING MY CLAS
APPLE BLACK

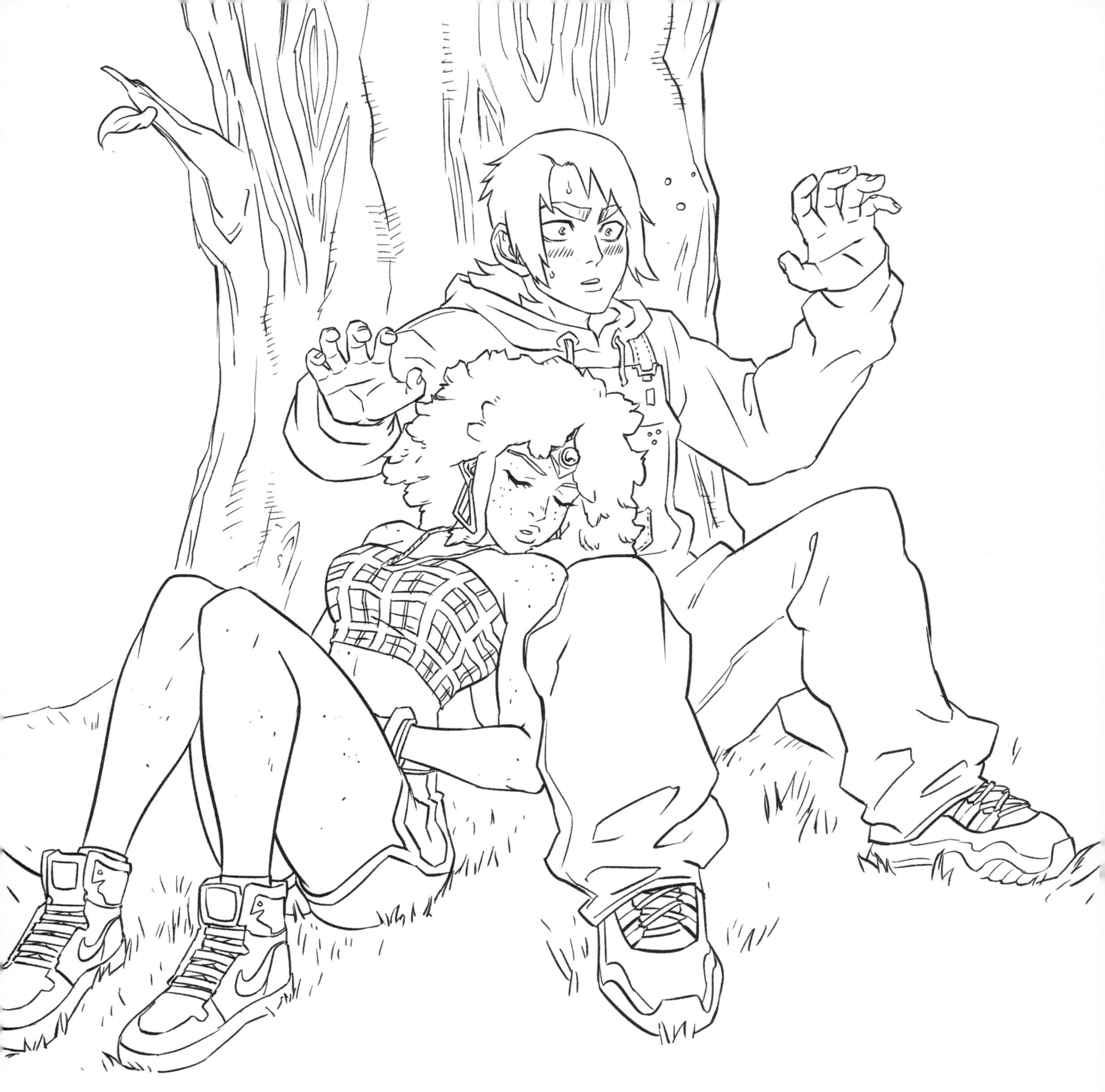

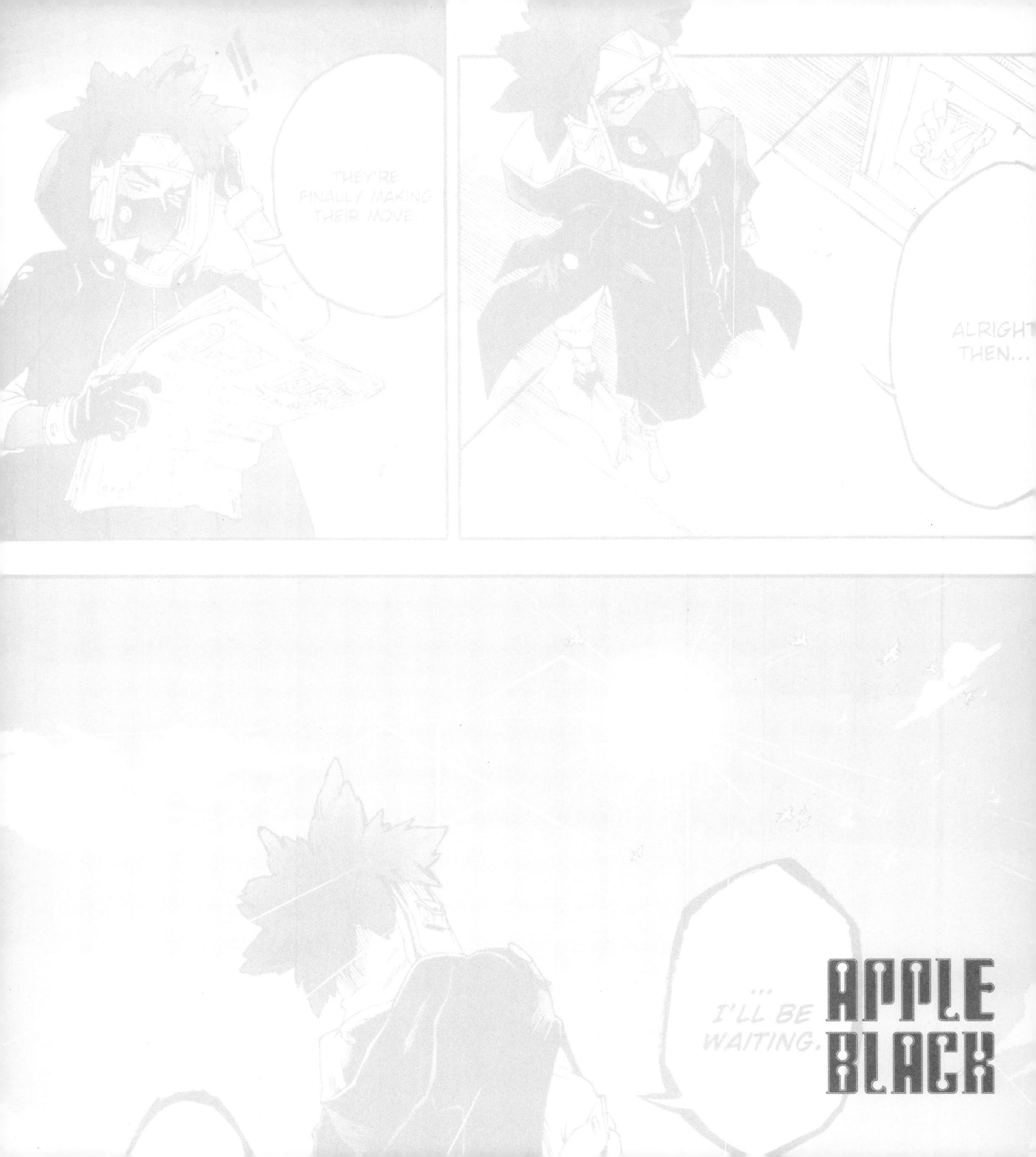
THEY'RE FINALLY MAKING THEIR MOVE.
ALRIGHT THEN...
... I'LL BE WAITING.
APPLE BLACK

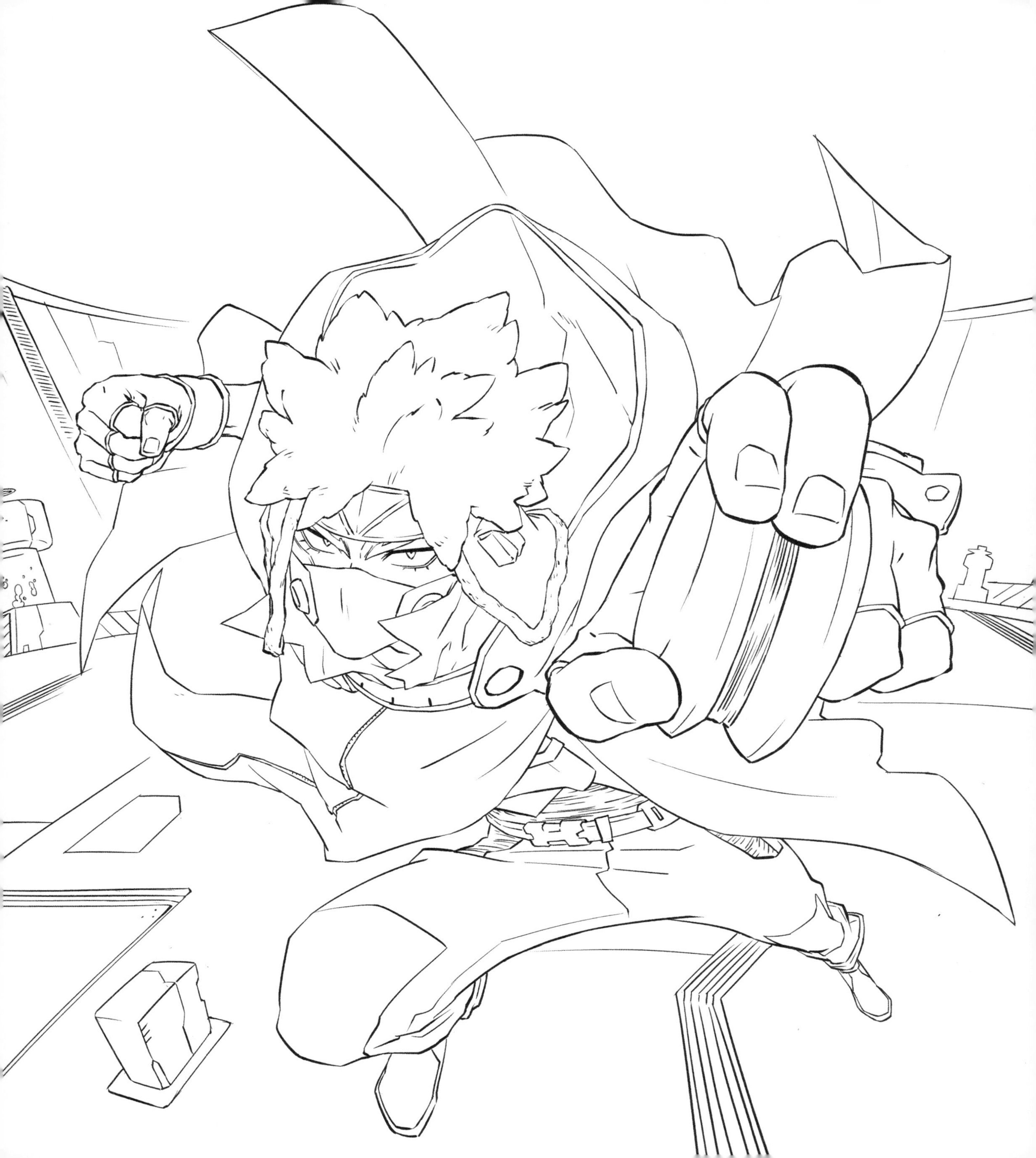

APPLE
BLACK

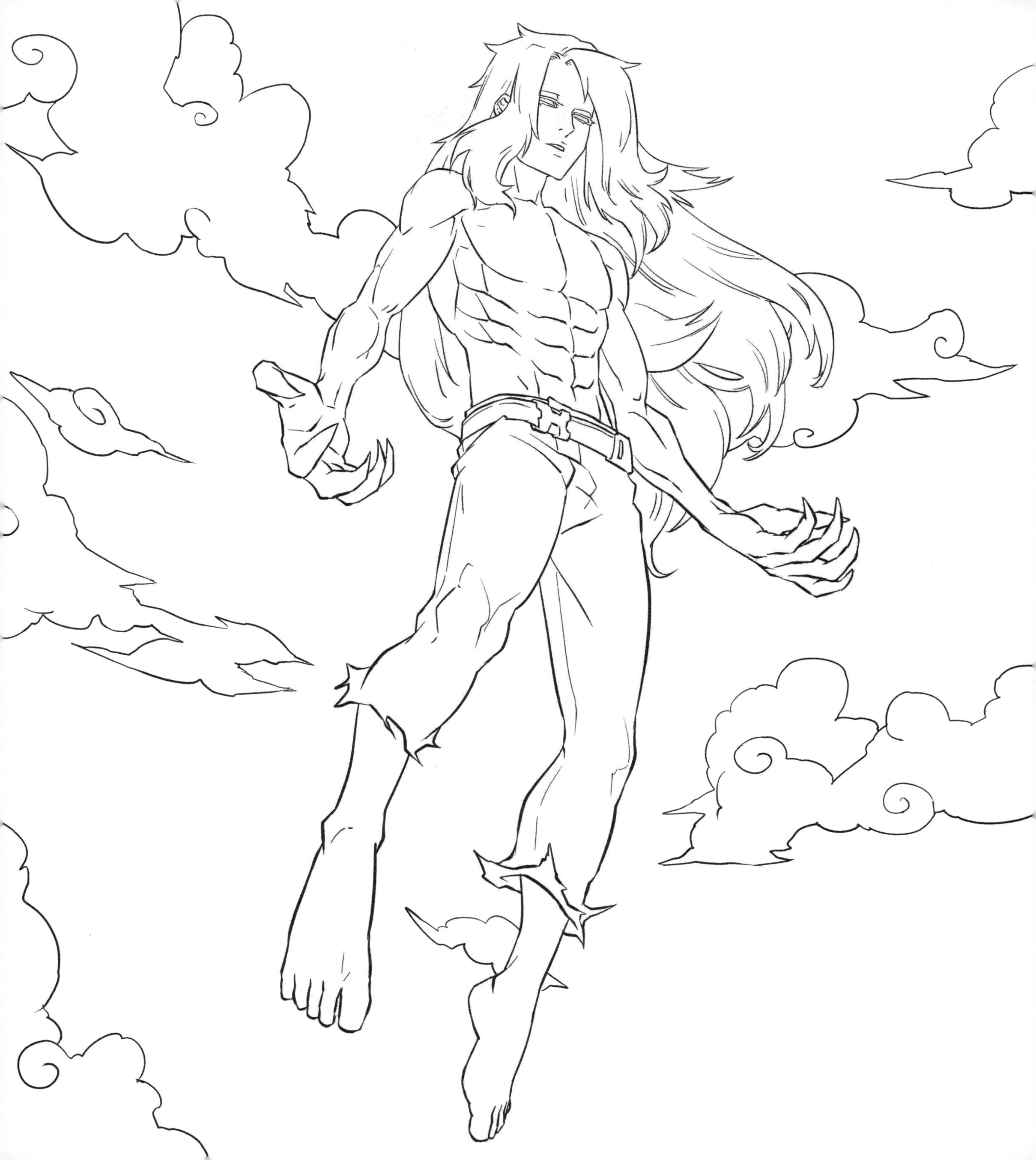

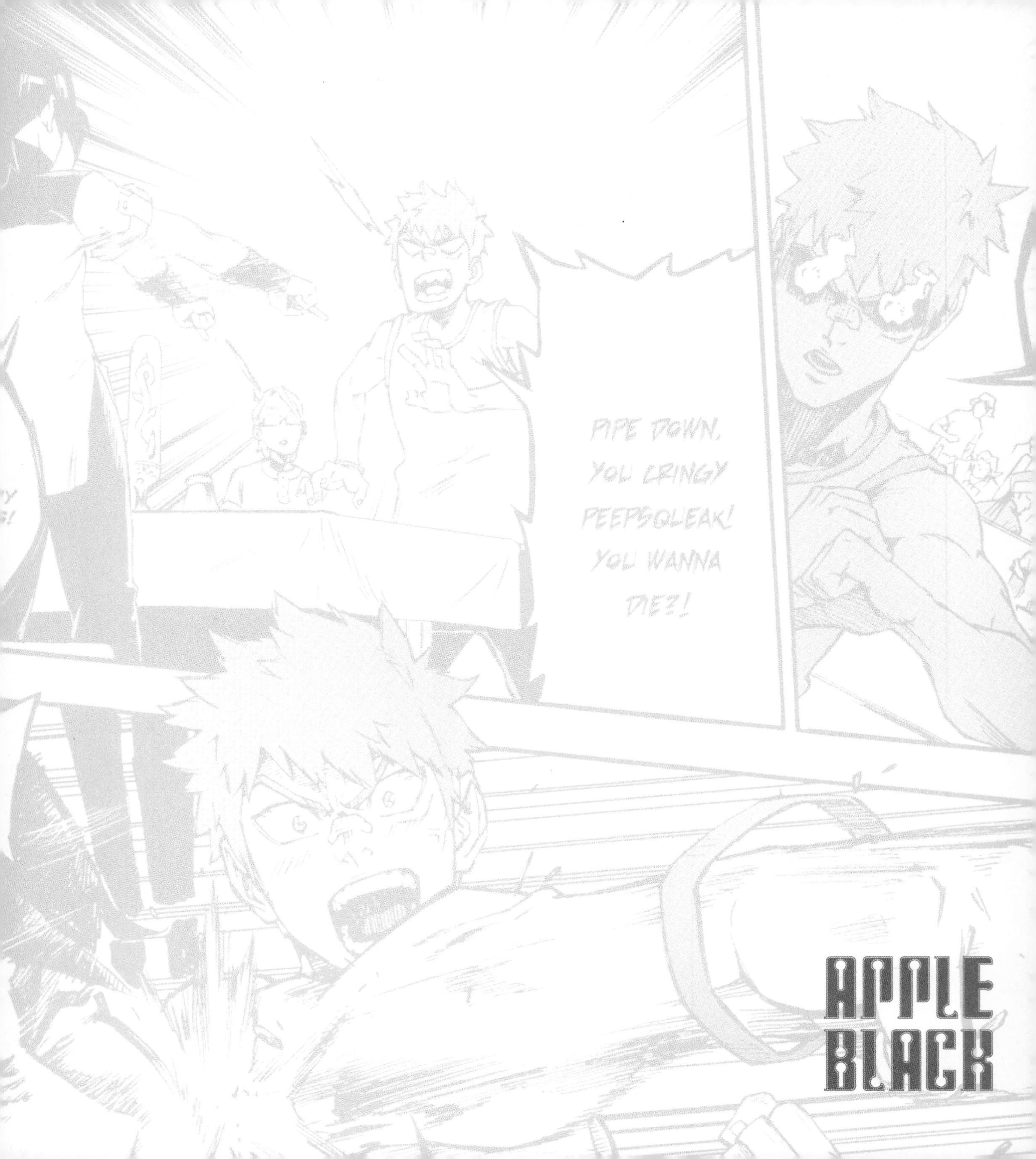
PIPE DOWN, YOU CRINGY PEEPSQUEAK! YOU WANNA DIE?!
APPLE BLACK

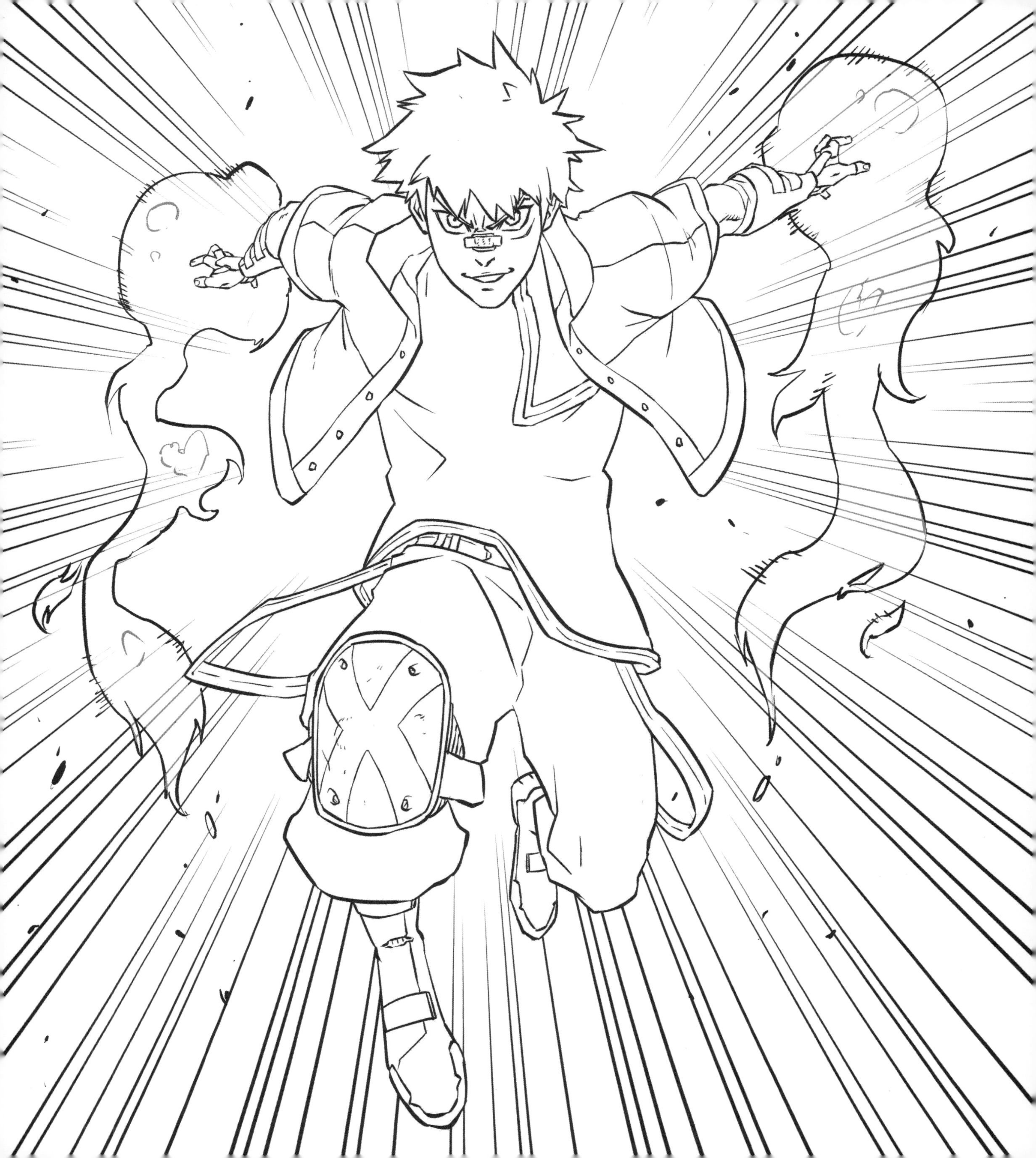

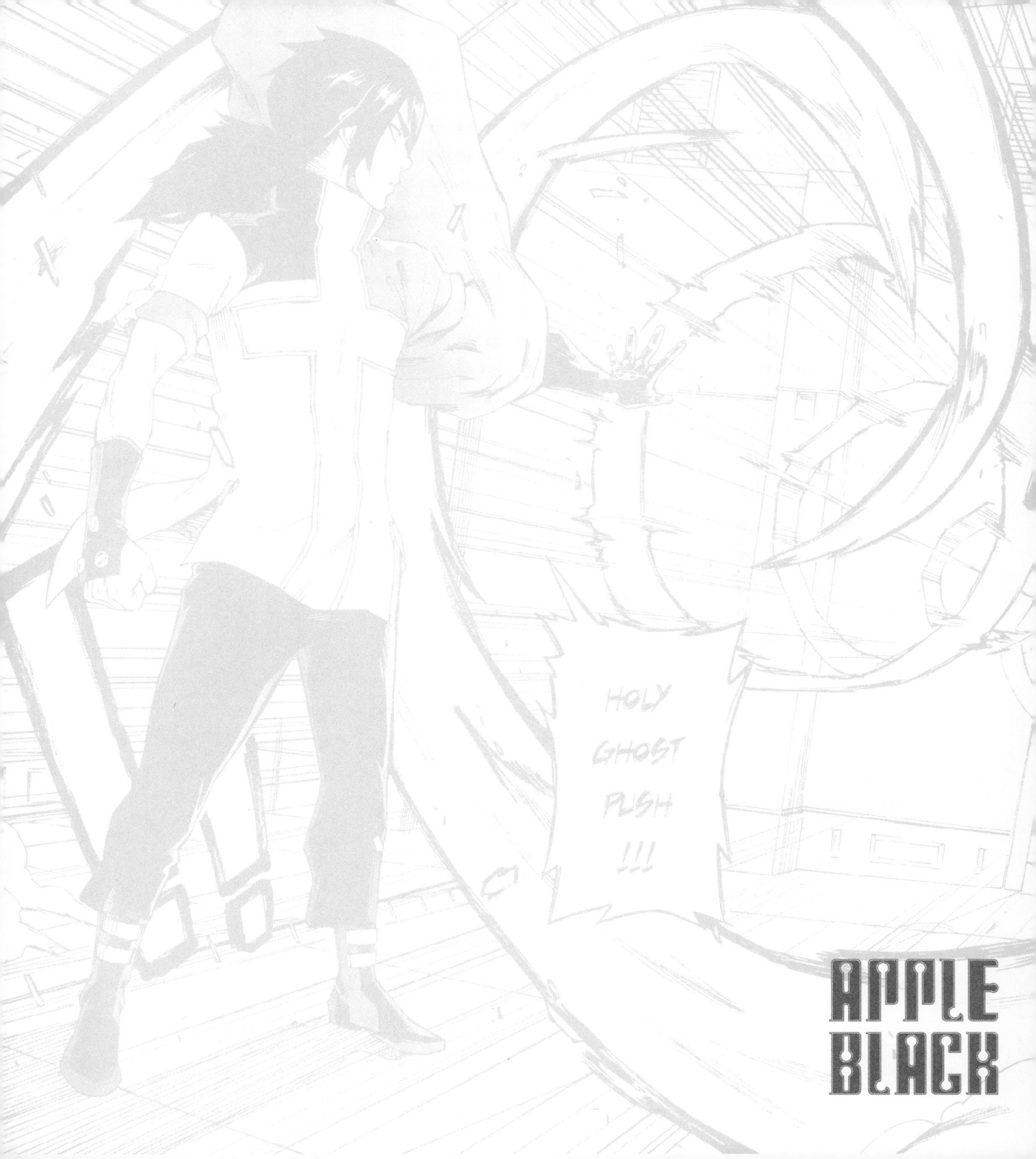
HOLY
GHOST
PUSH
!!!
APPLE
BLACK

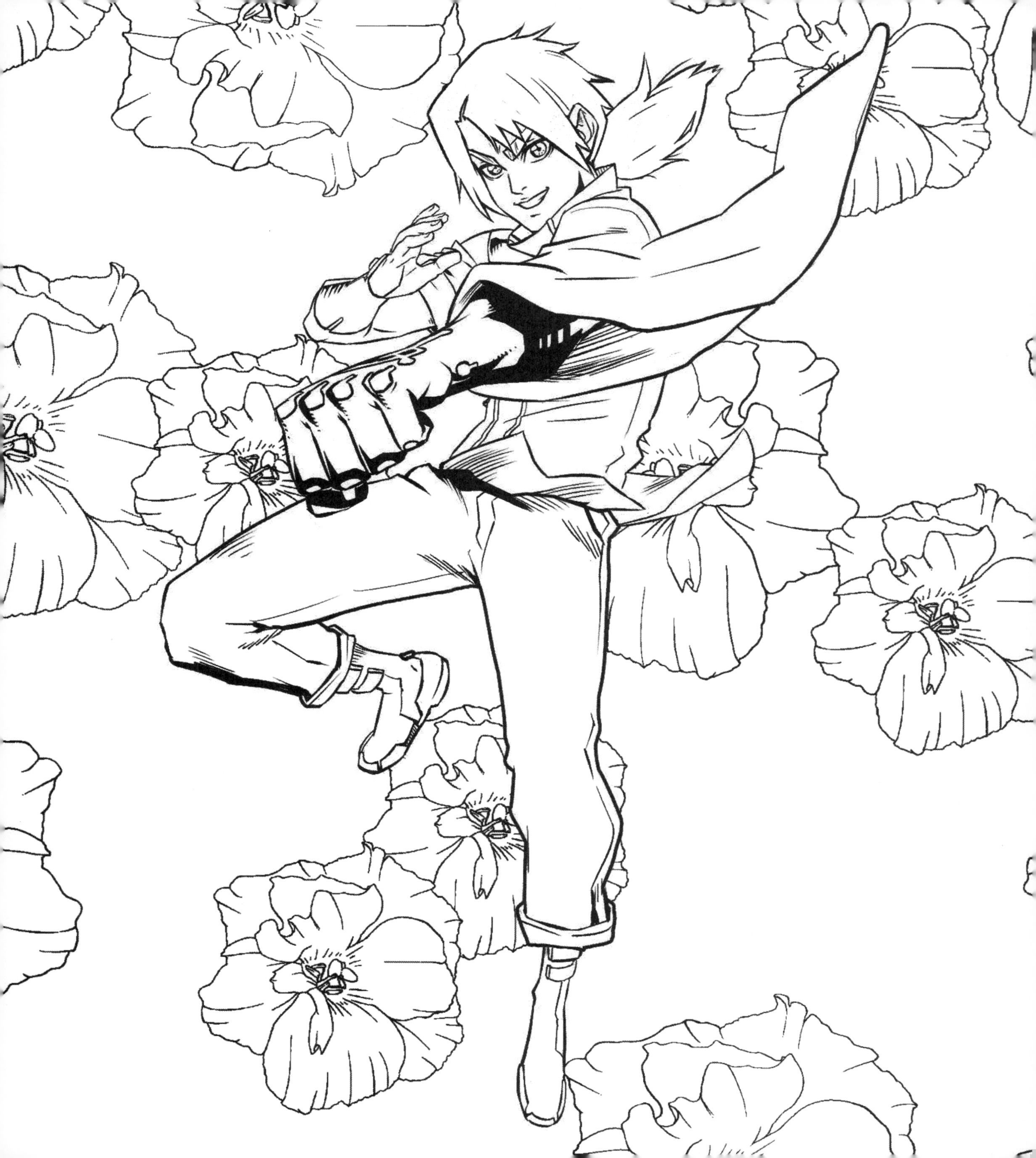

APPLE
BLACK

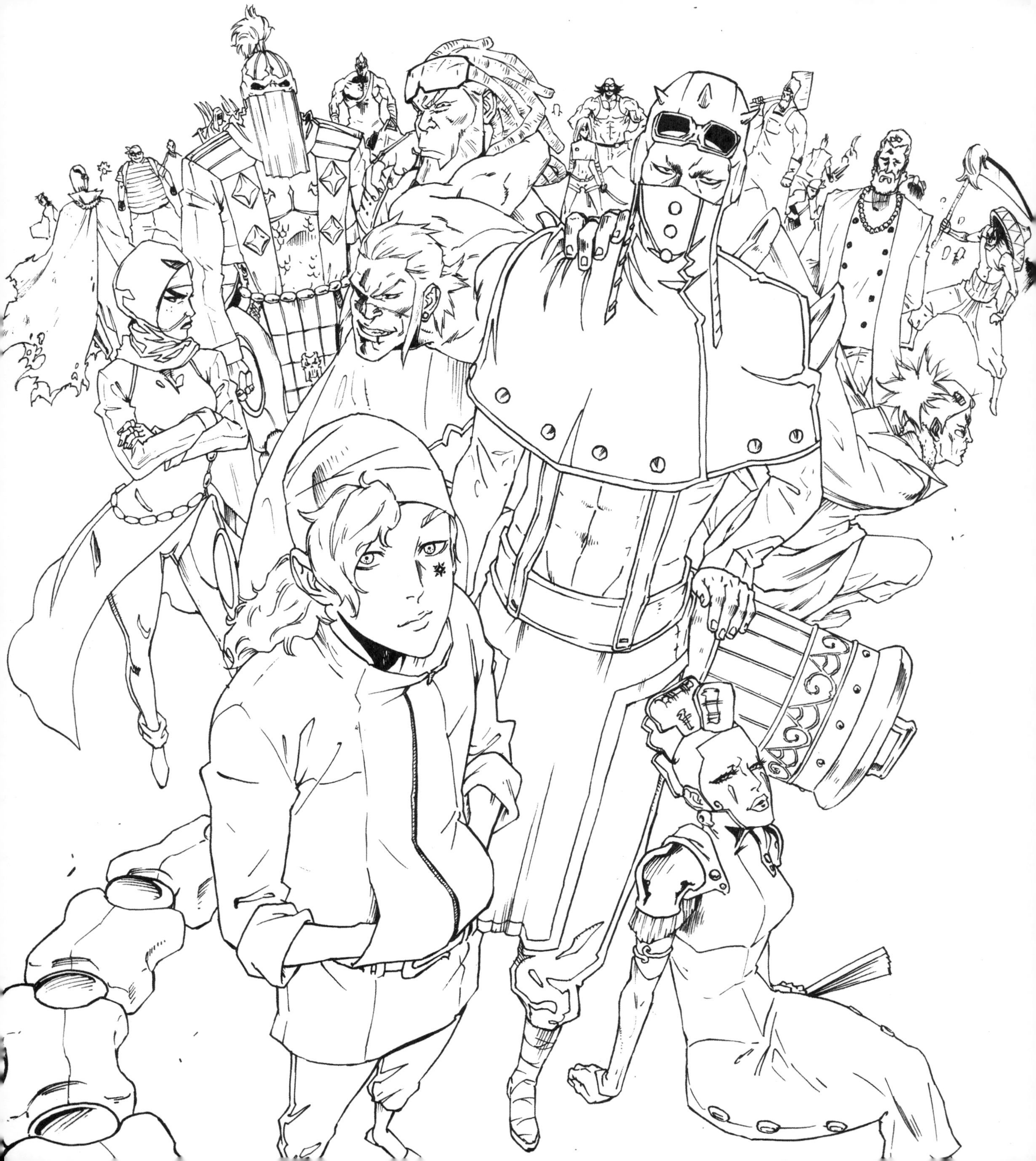

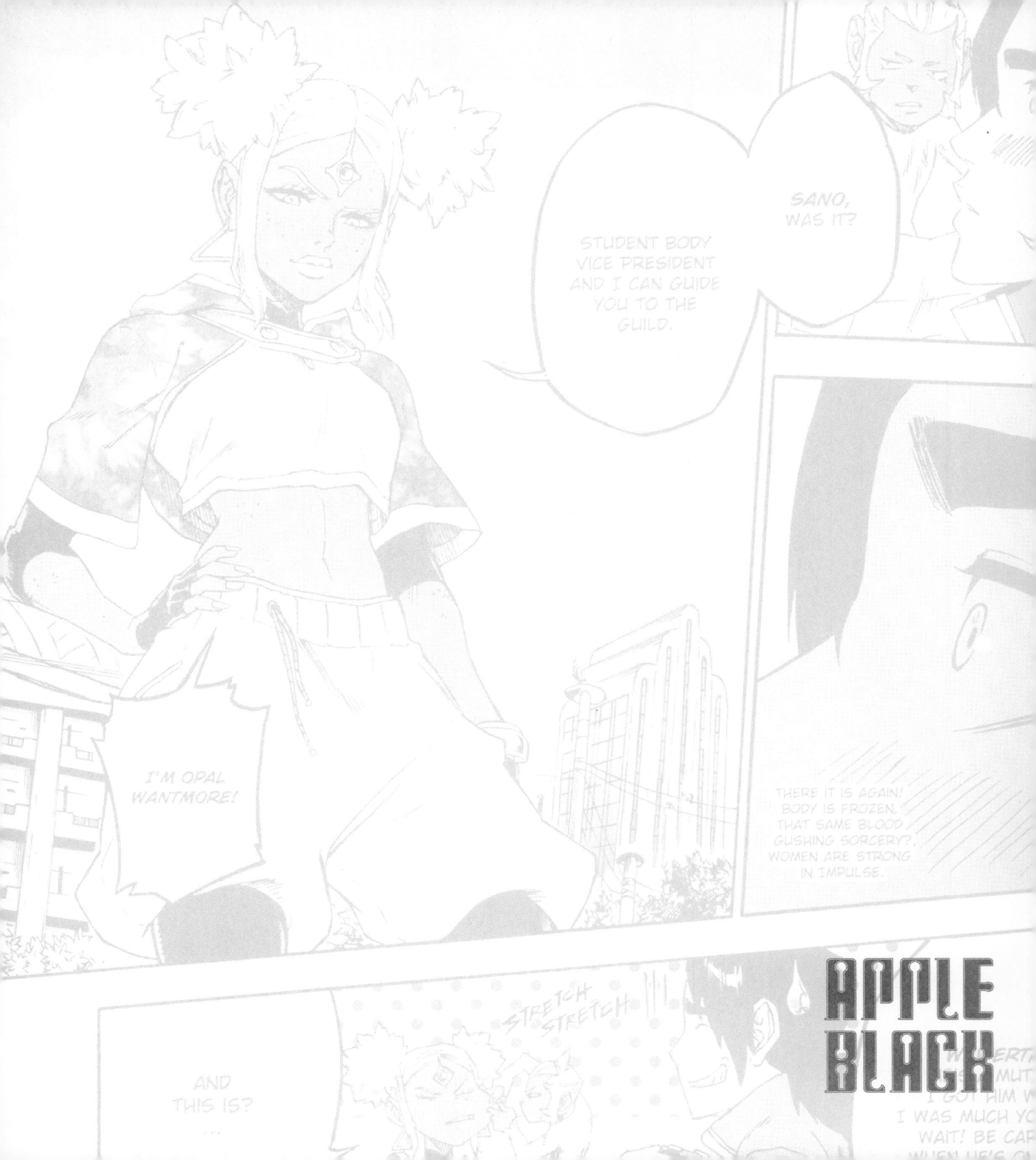
I'M OPAL WANTMORE!
STUDENT BODY VICE PRESIDENT AND I CAN GUIDE YOU TO THE GUILD.
SANO, WAS IT?
THERE IT IS AGAIN! BODY IS FROZEN. THAT SAME BLOOD GUSHING SORCERY?. WOMEN ARE STRONG IN IMPULSE.
STRETCH STRETCH
AND THIS IS? ...
APPLE BLACK
WAIT! BE CA

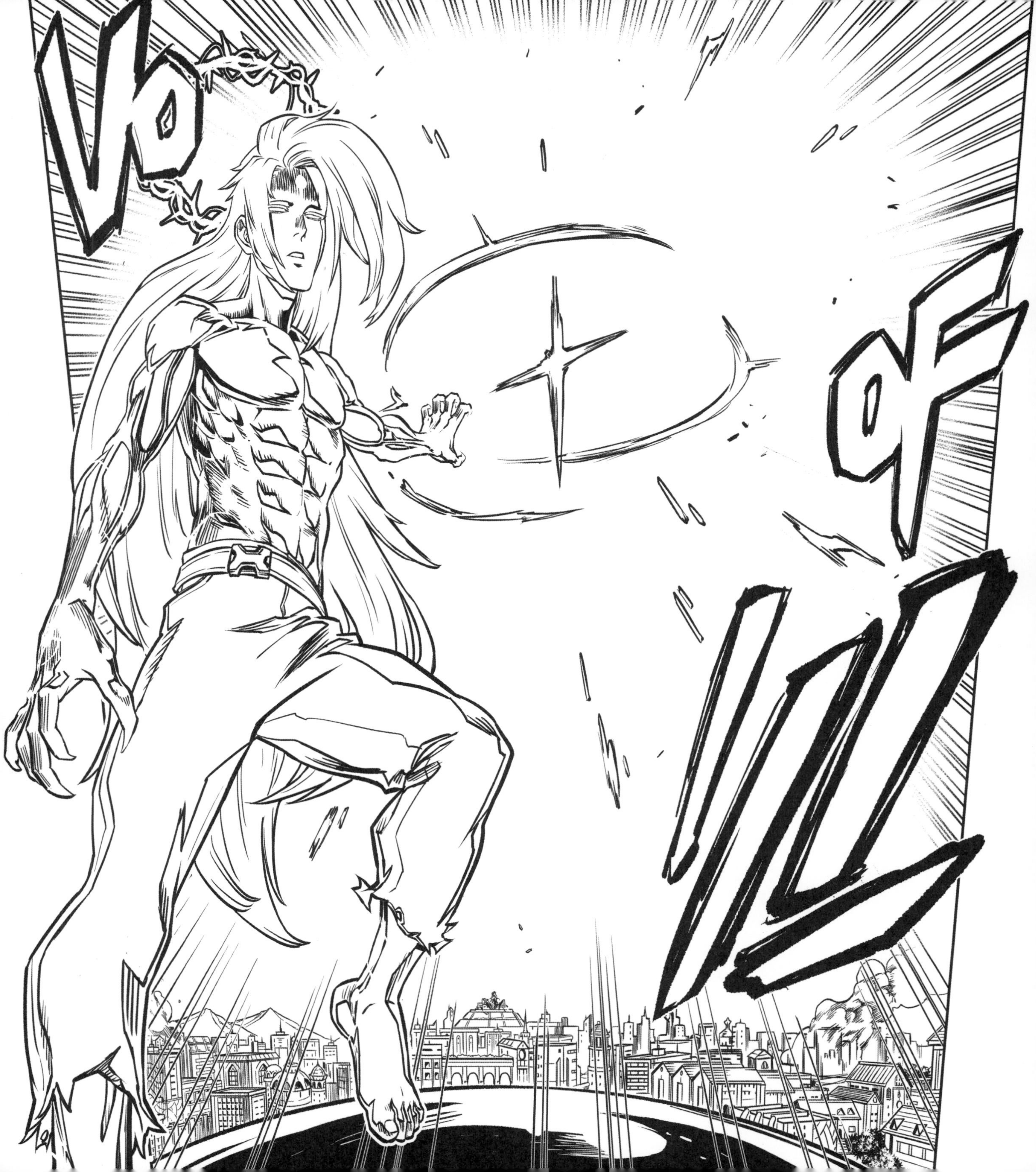

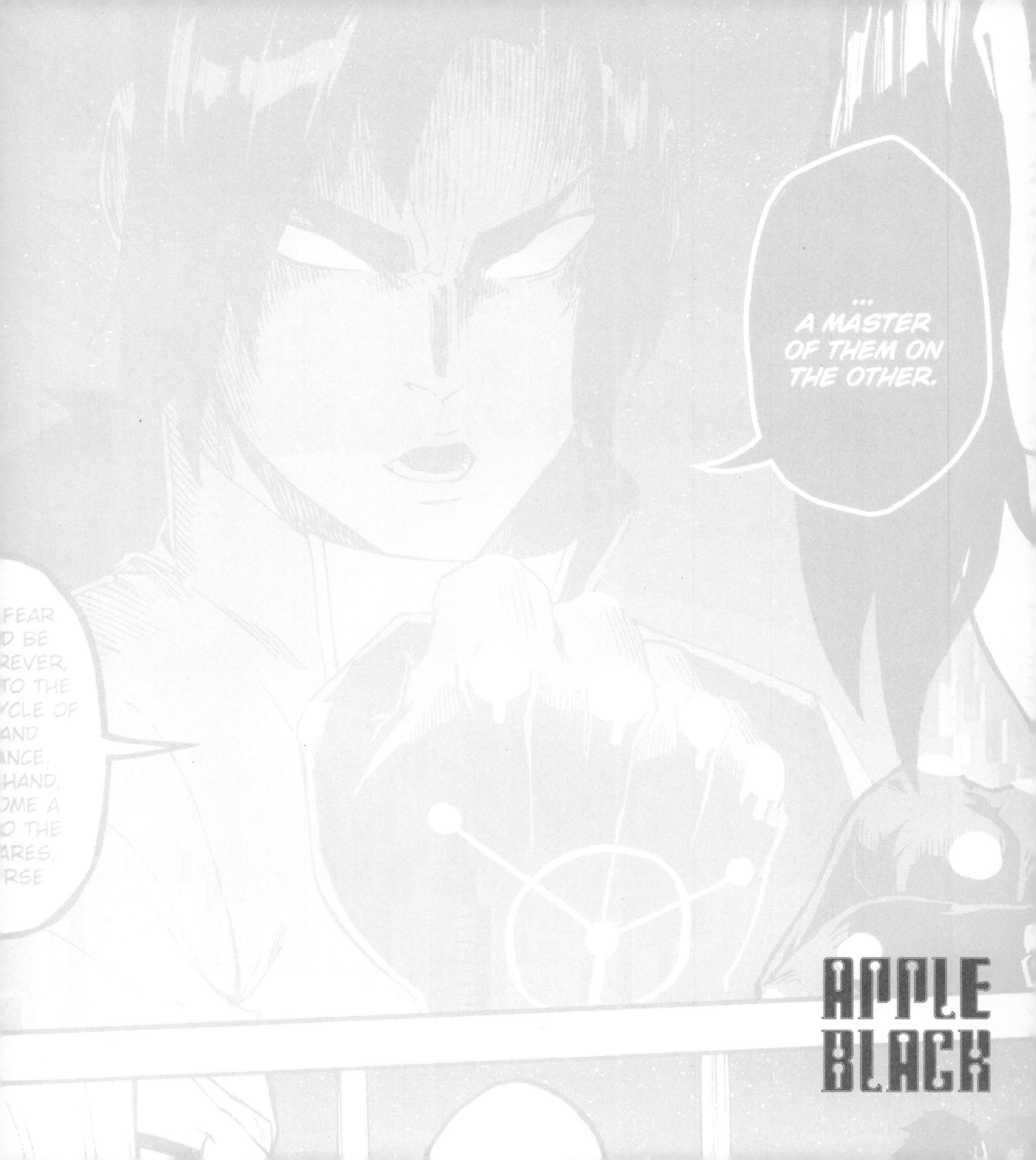
... A MASTER OF THEM ON THE OTHER.
APPLE BLACK

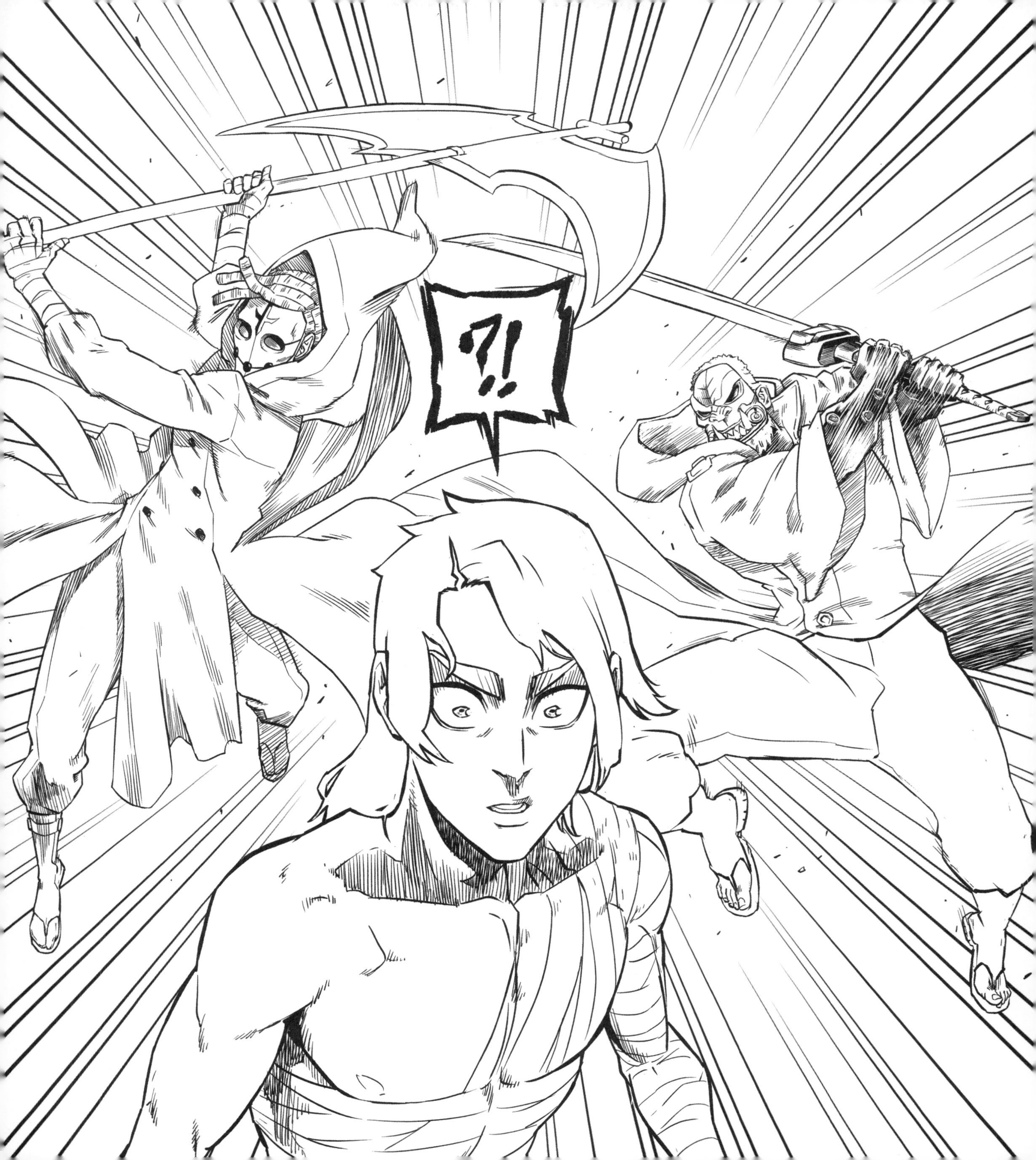
?!!

APPLE
BLACK

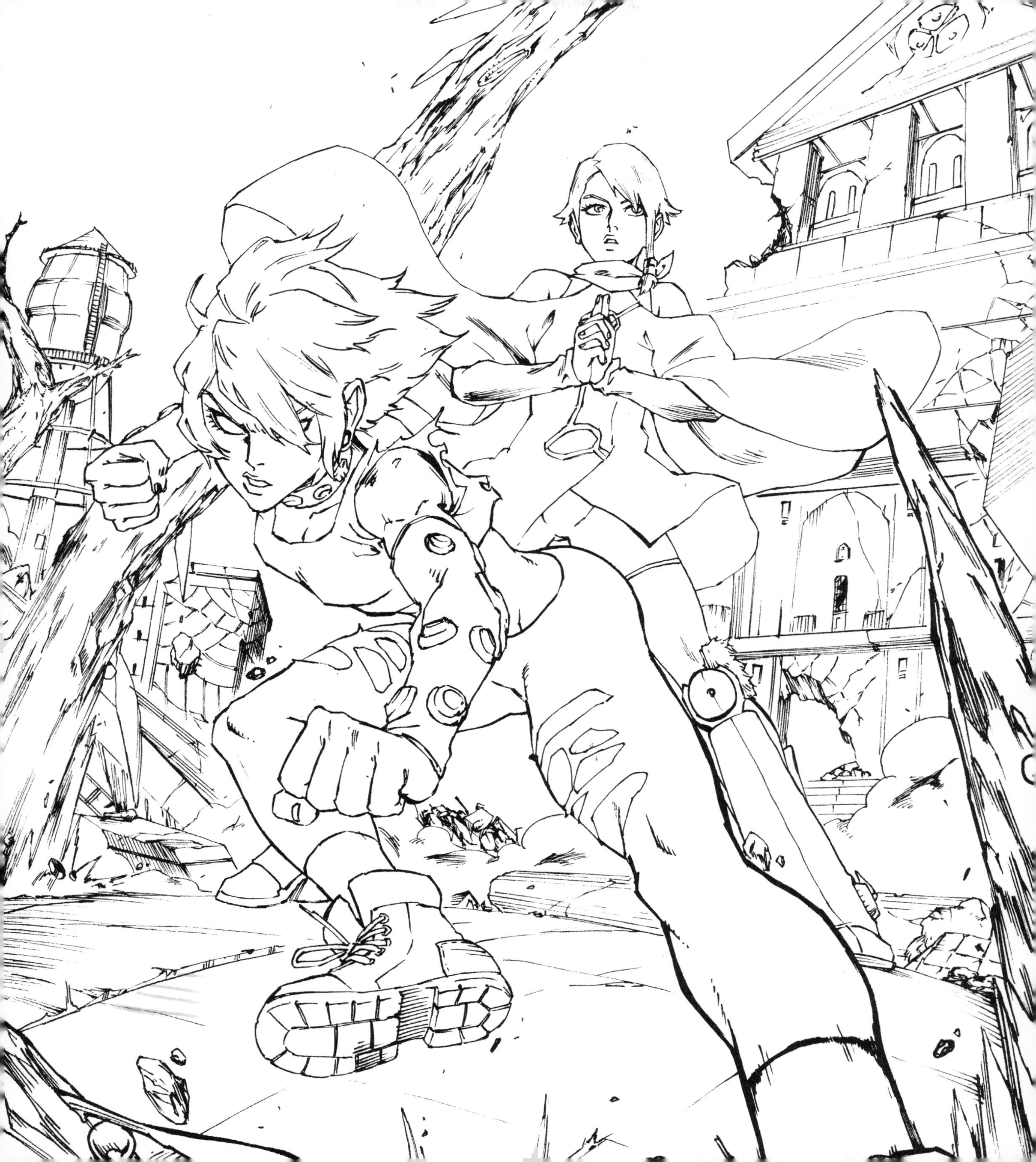

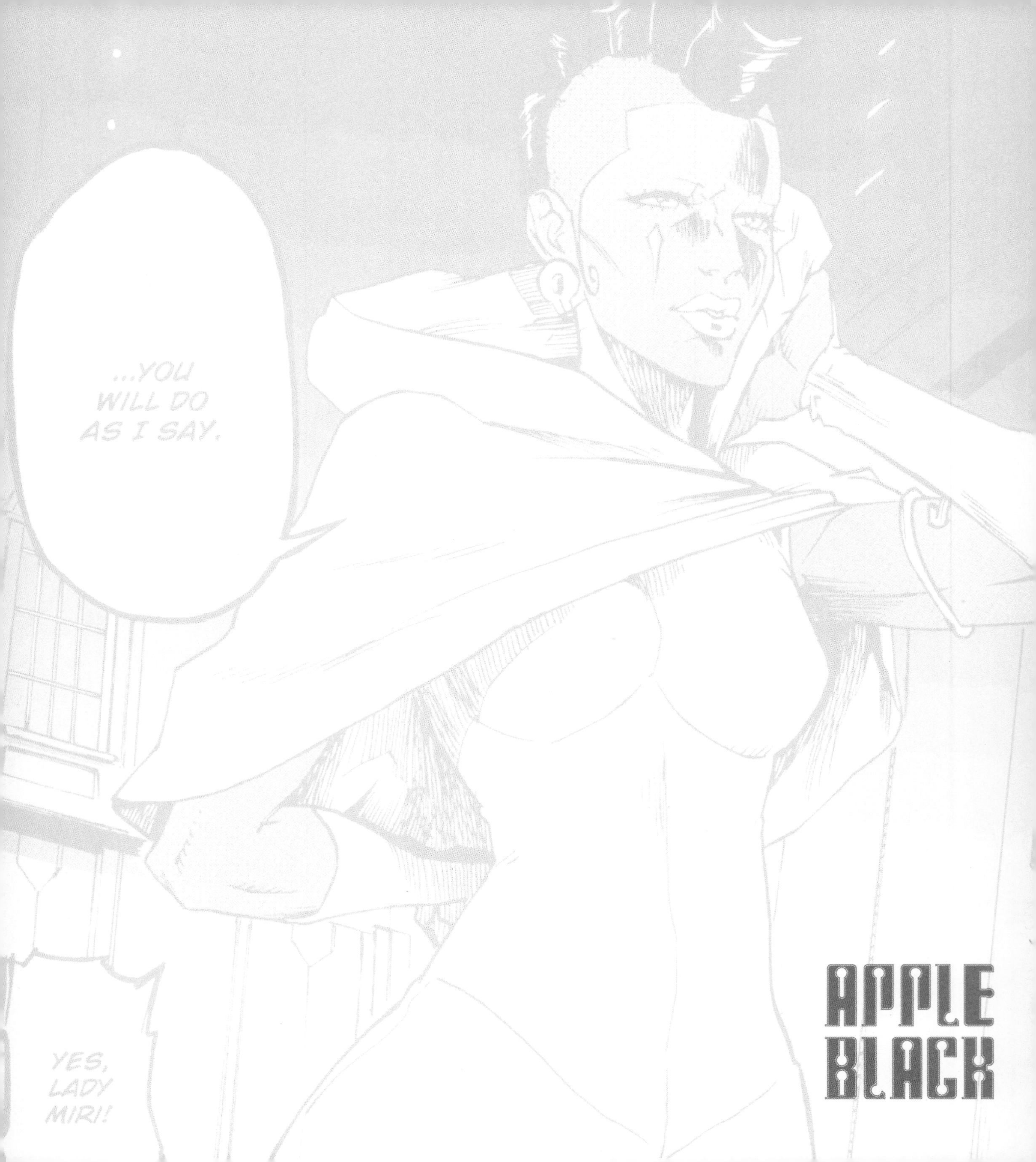
...YOU WILL DO AS I SAY.
YES, LADY MIRI!
APPLE BLACK

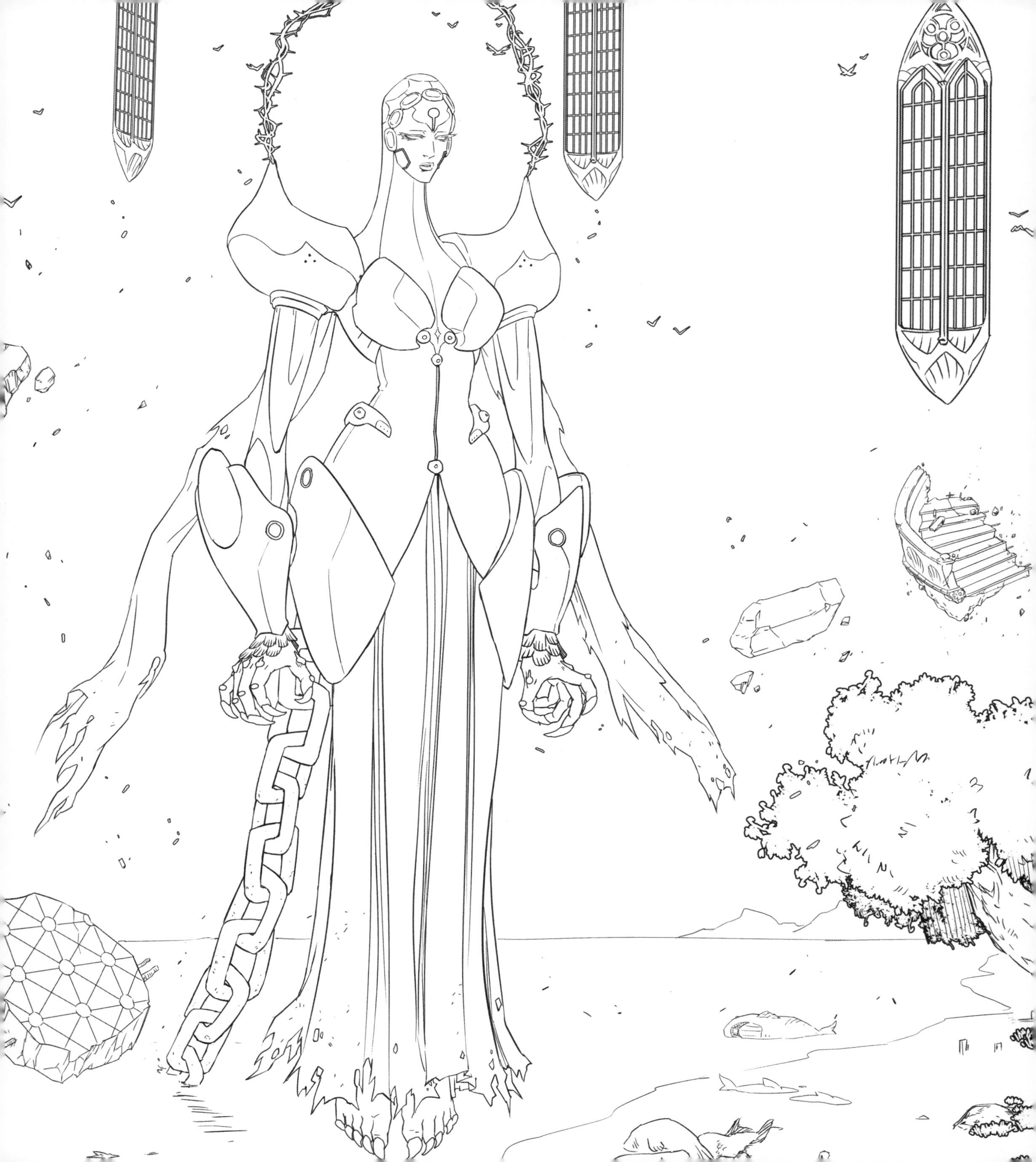

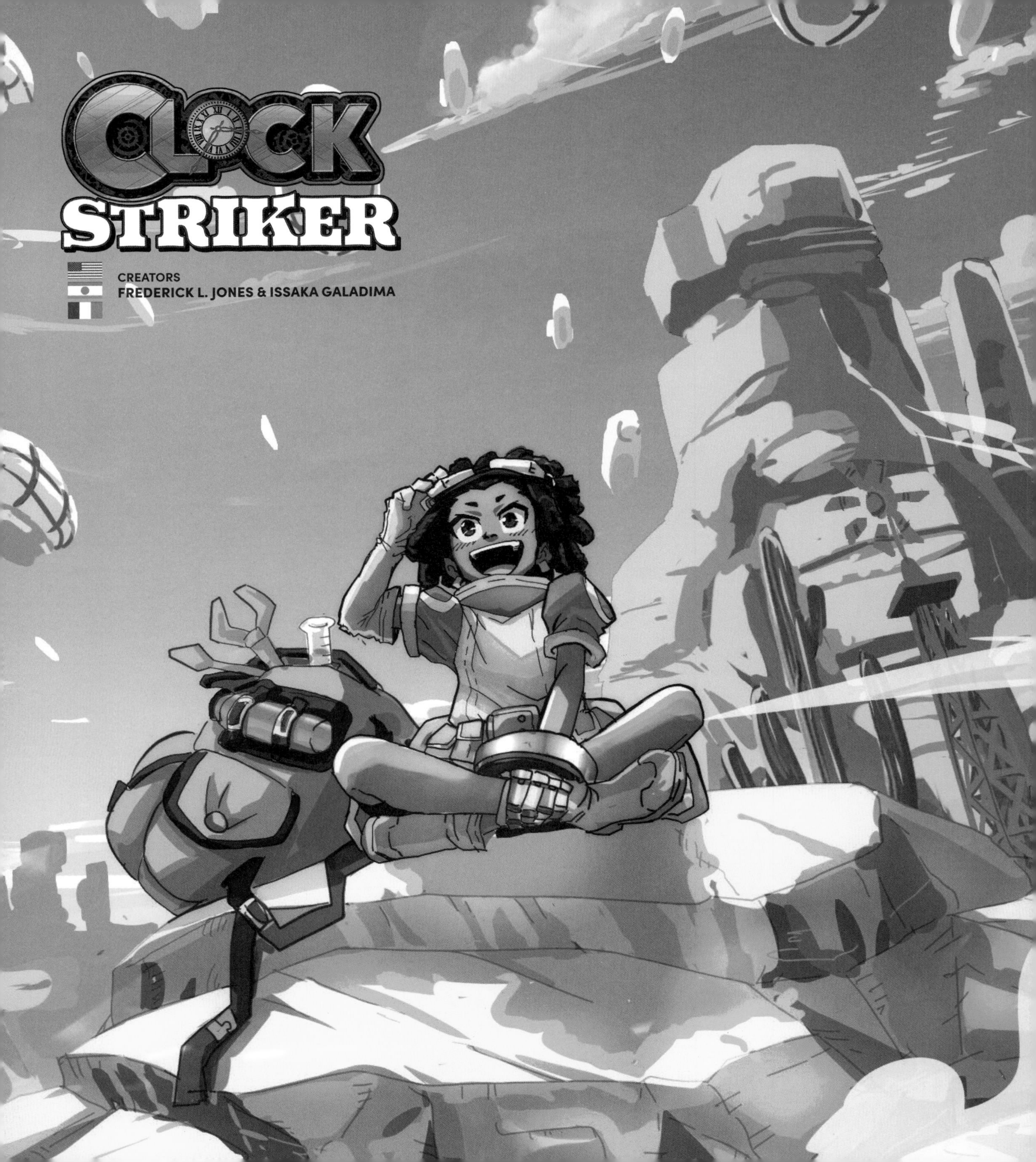
CLOCK
STRIKER
CREATORS
FREDERICK L. JONES & ISSAKA GALADIMA

CAST

NAME: CAST IRONS

HEIGHT: 5'3"

SERIES: CLOCK STRIKER

BIO: Exceptionally smart and scrappy, Cast is capable of building almost anything she can think of. Her greatest invention is her MOBILE LAB prosthetic hand, which can conduct chemical experiments, fire metallic fingers, produce a grappling hook, and discharge a thousand volts of electricity!

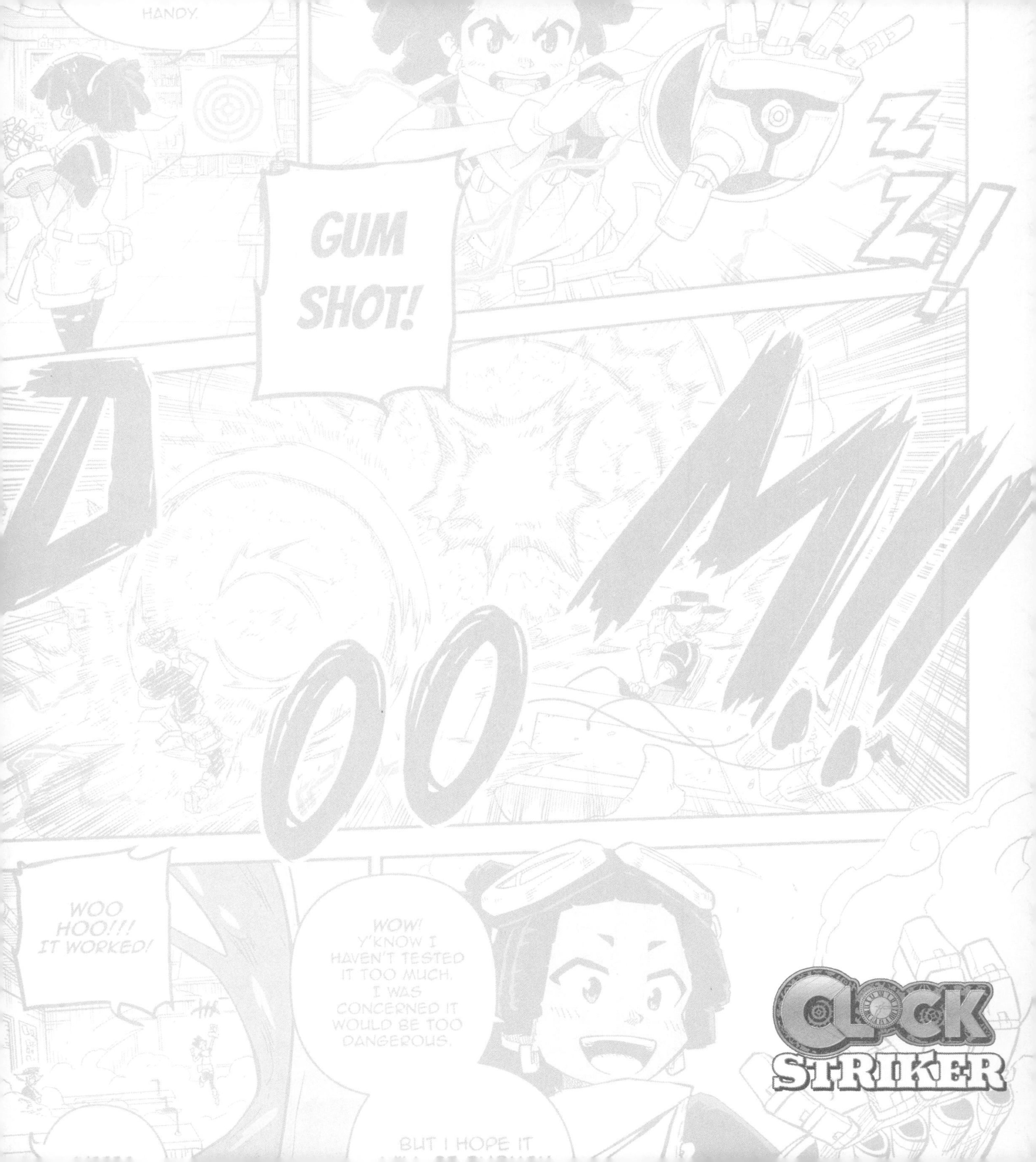
HANDY.
GUM SHOT!
ZZ!
DOOM!!
WOO HOO!!! IT WORKED!
WOW! Y'KNOW I HAVEN'T TESTED IT TOO MUCH. I WAS CONCERNED IT WOULD BE TOO DANGEROUS.
BUT I HOPE IT
CLOCK STRIKER

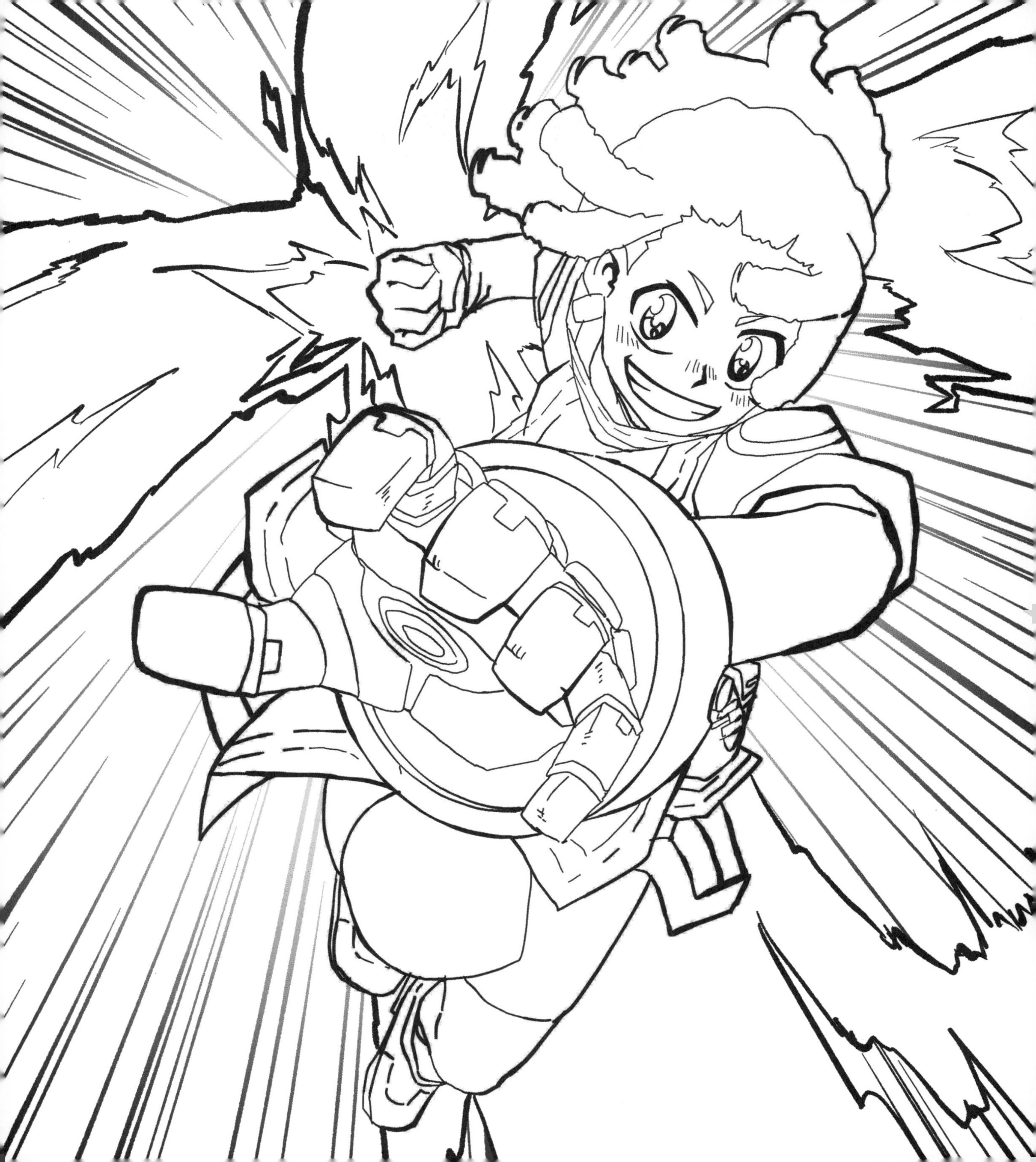

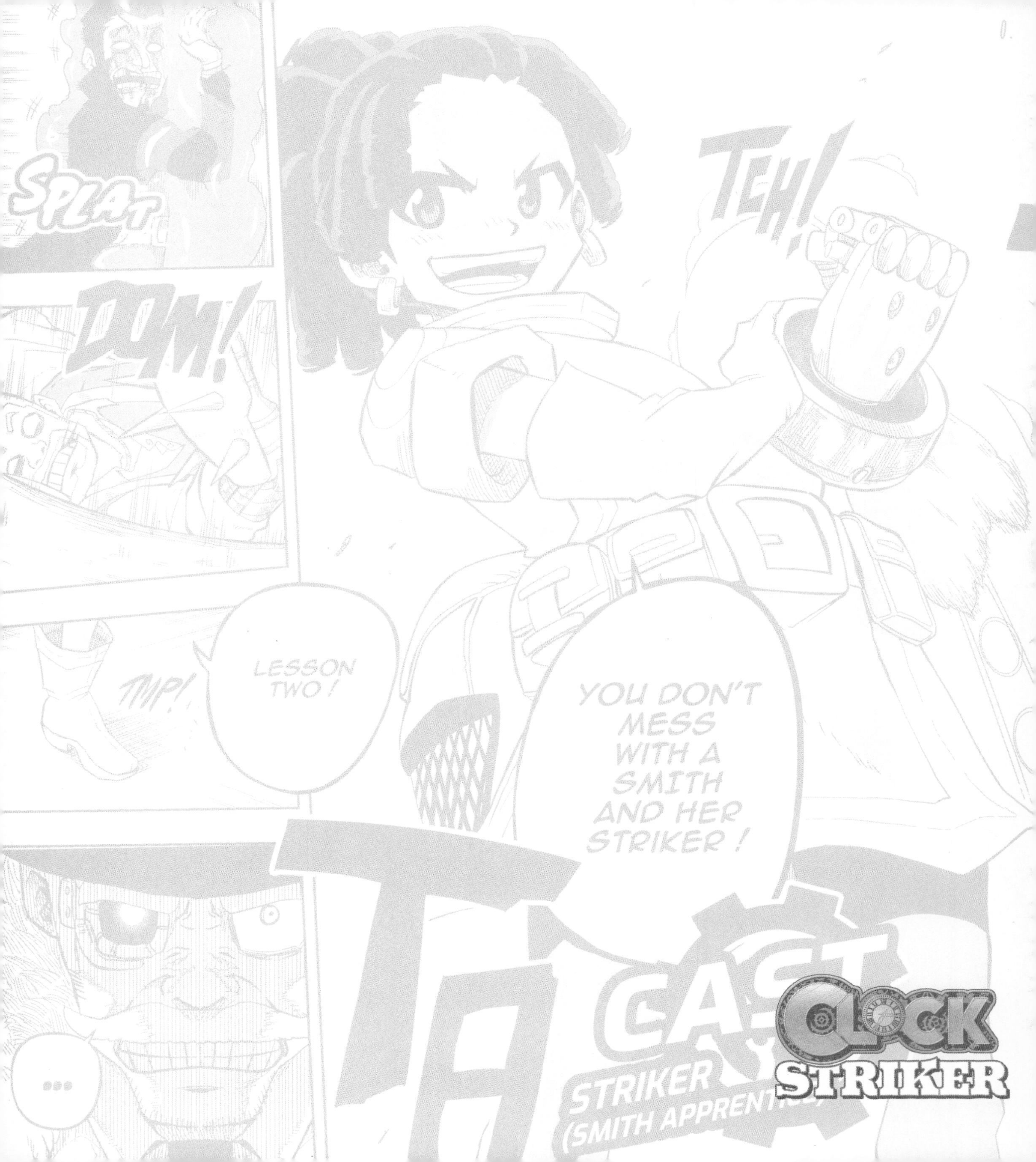
SPLAT
DOOM!
TMP!
...
TCH!
LESSON TWO!
YOU DON'T MESS WITH A SMITH AND HER STRIKER!
CAST
STRIKER
CLOCK STRIKER

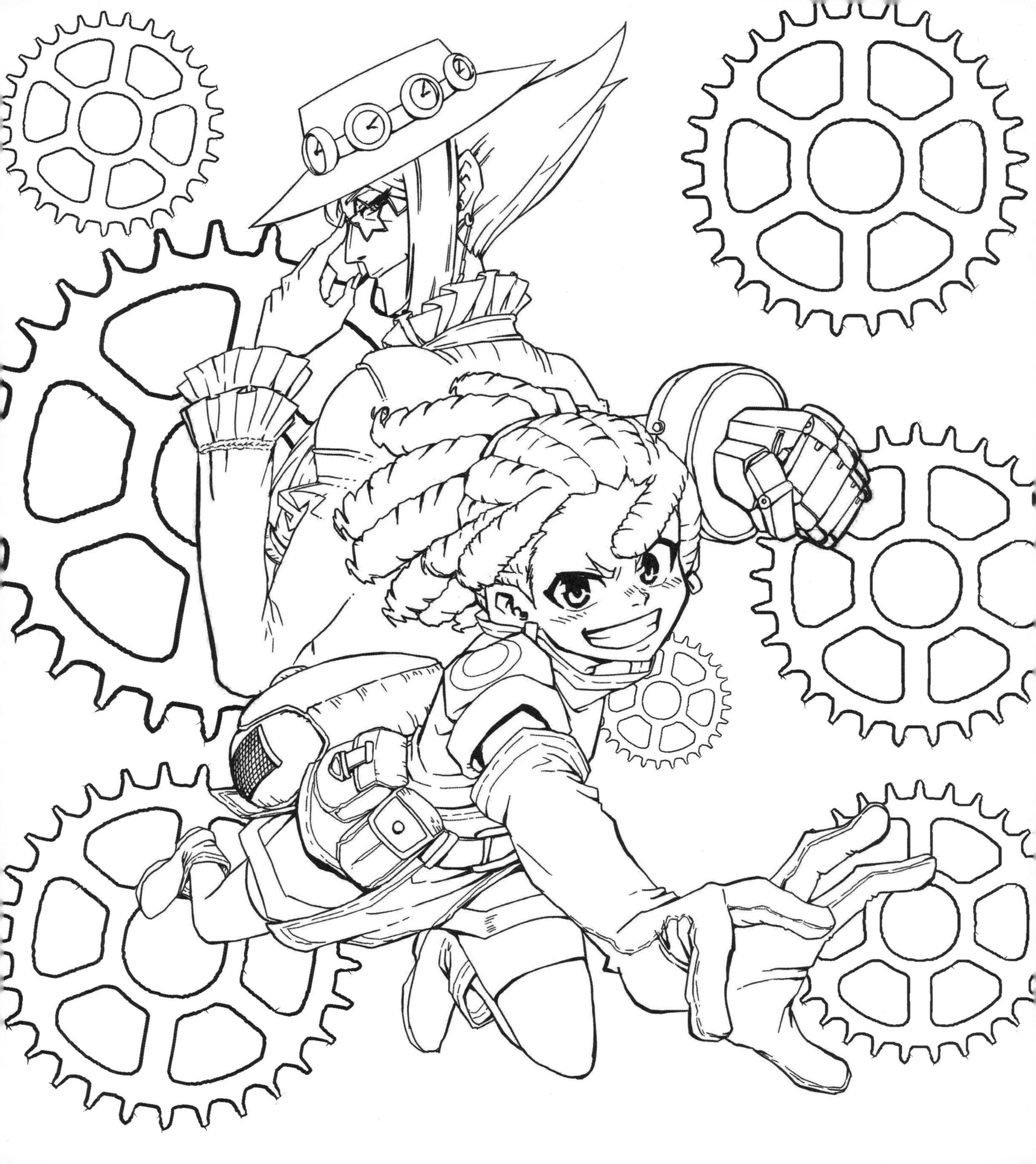

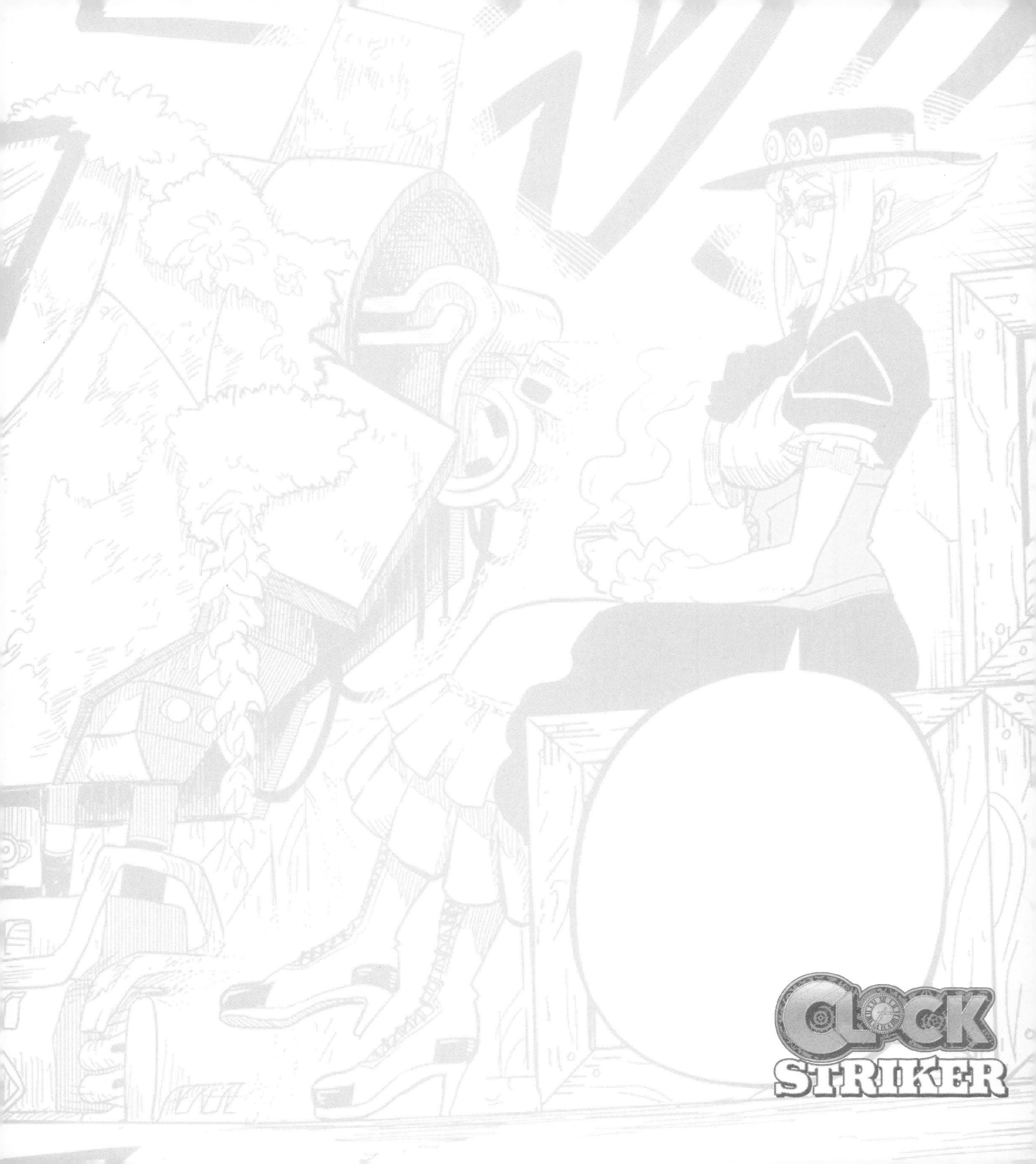
CLOCK
STRIKER

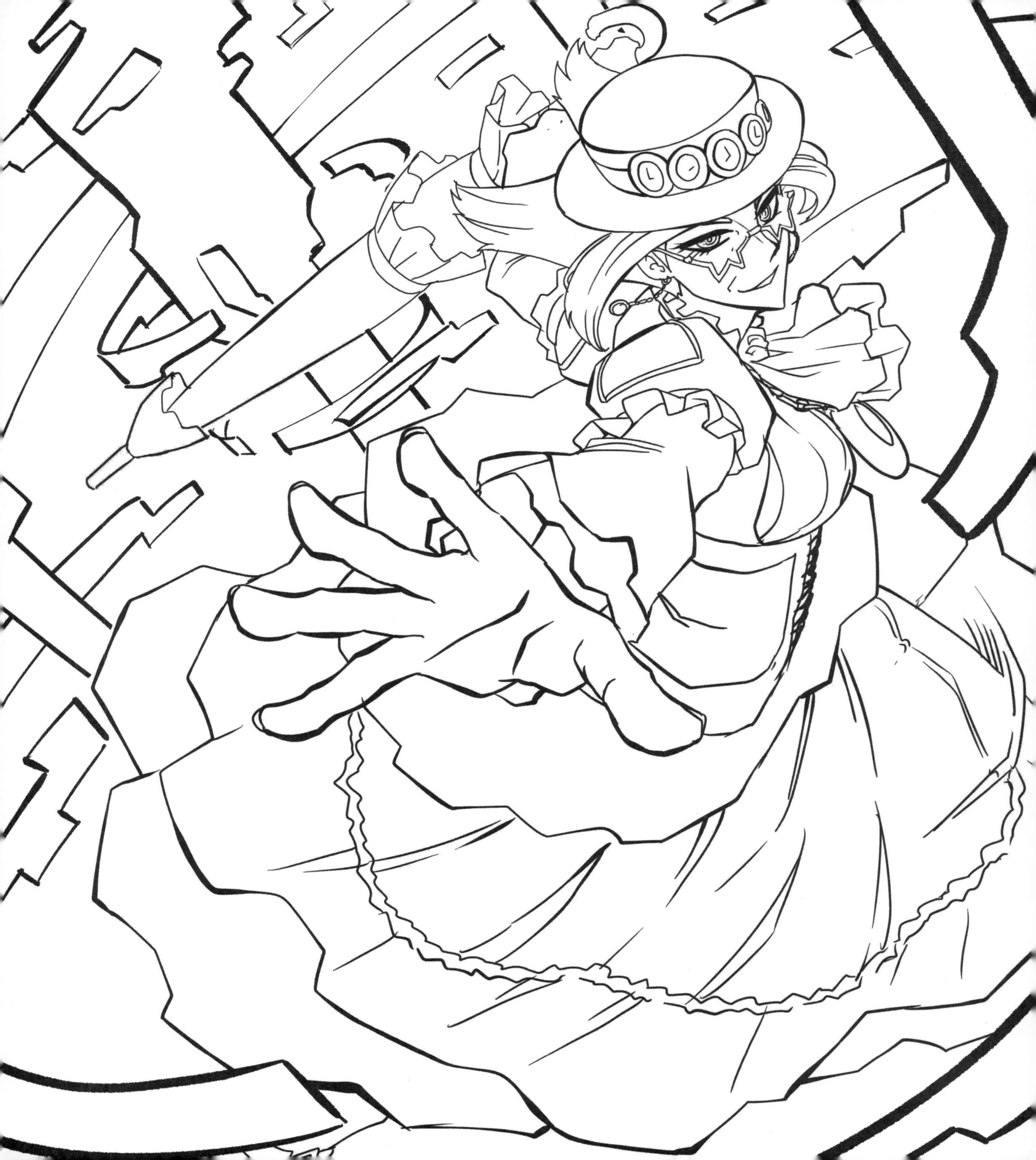

CLOCK STRIKER

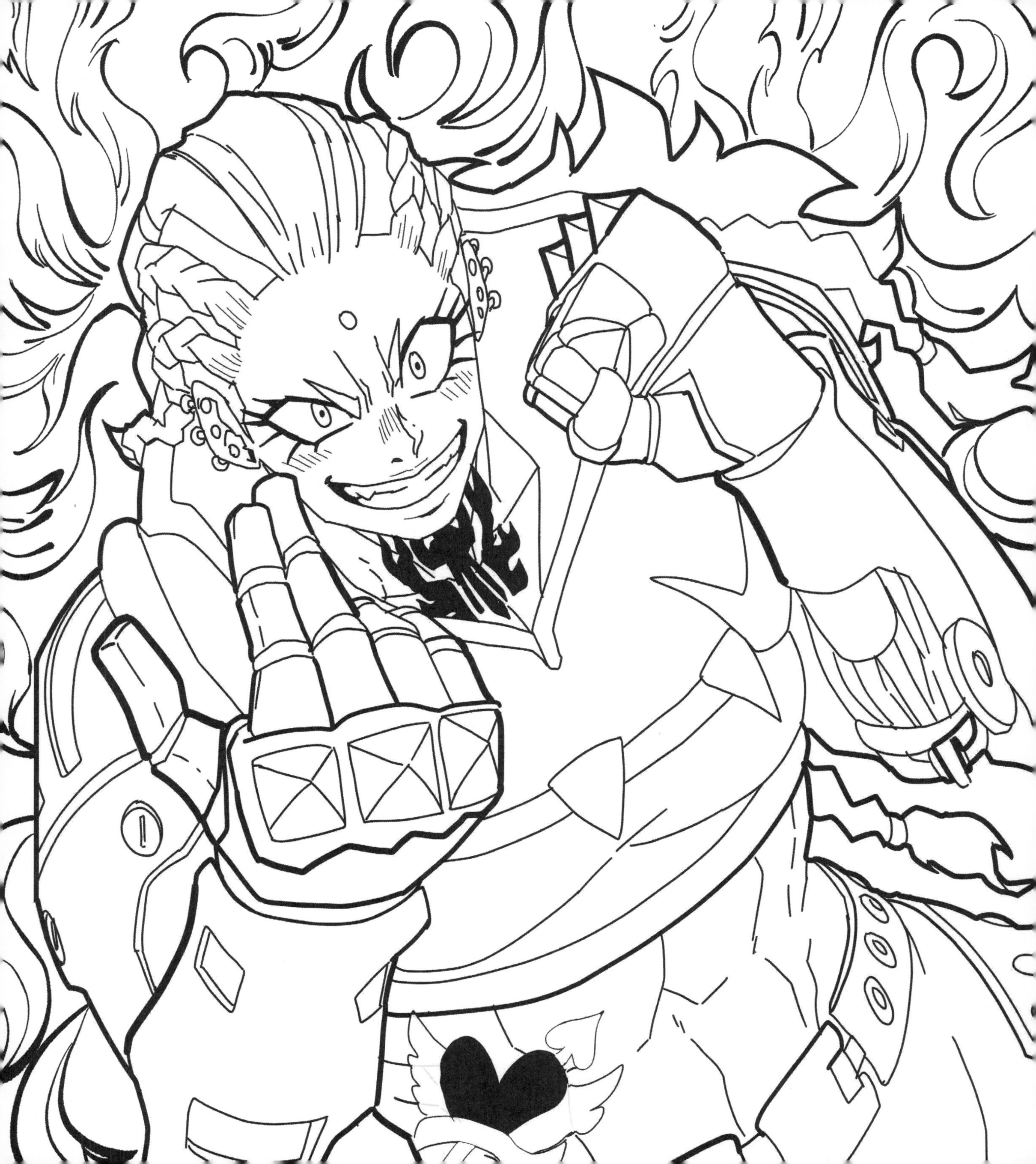

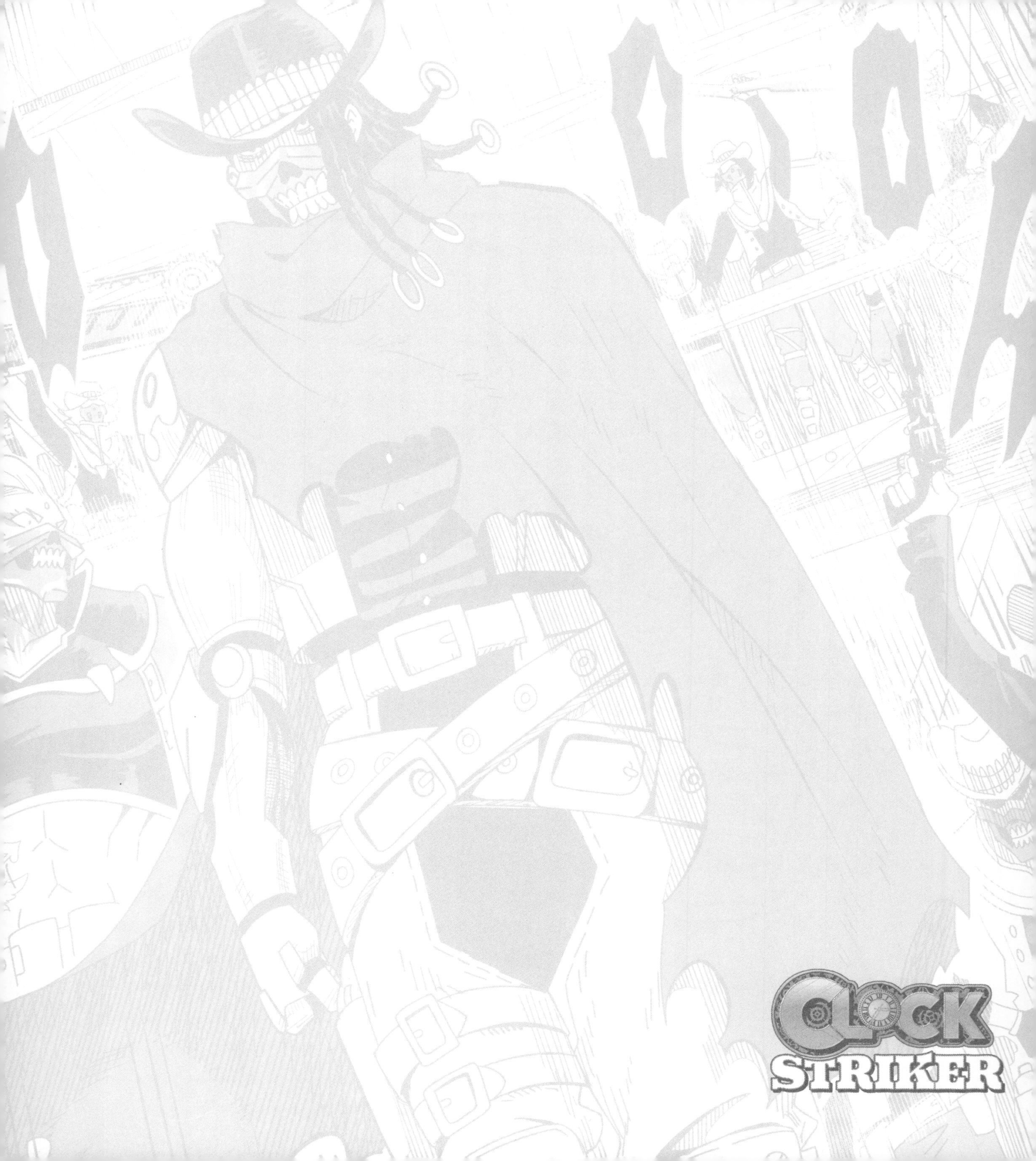
CLOCK
STRIKER

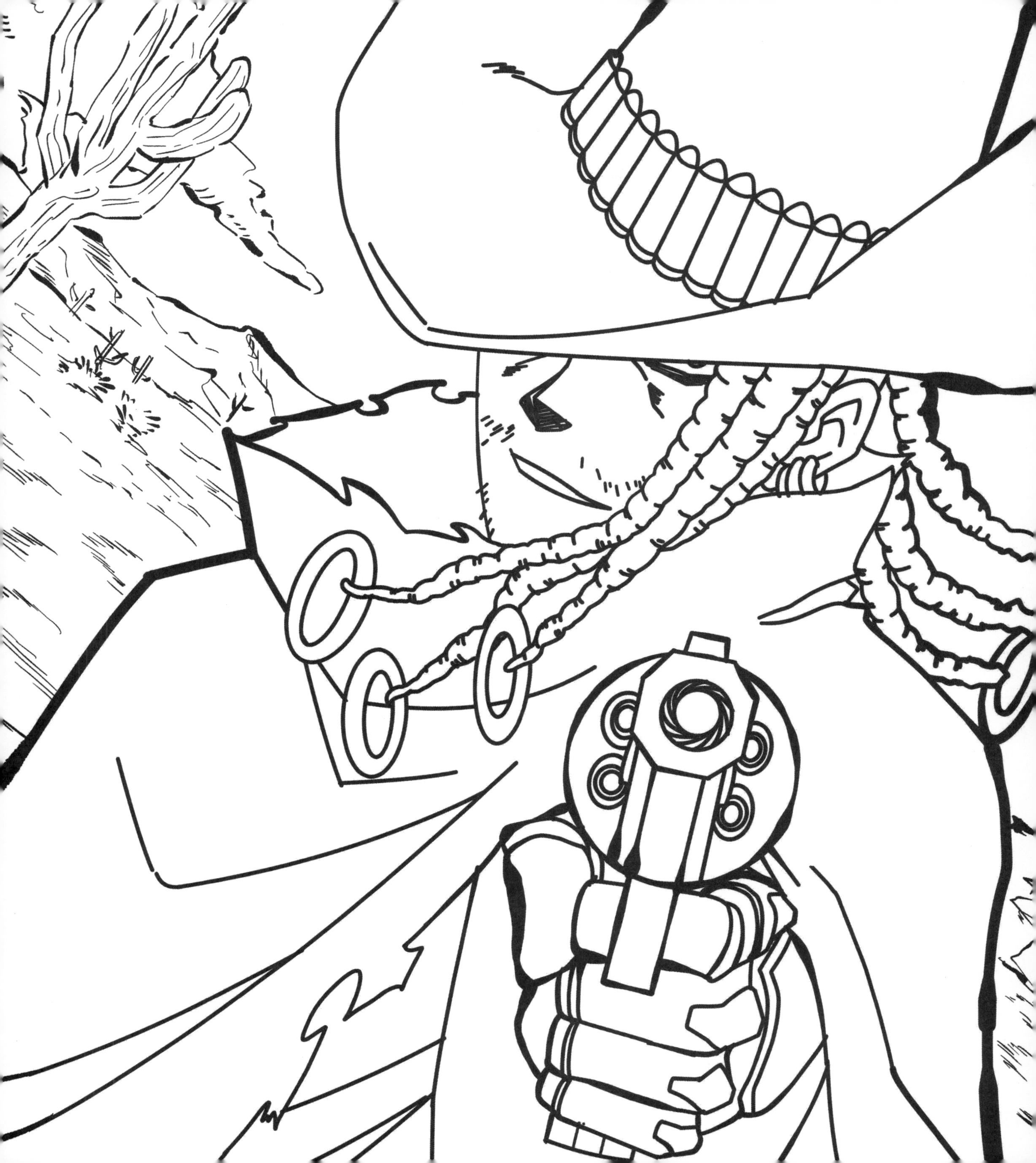

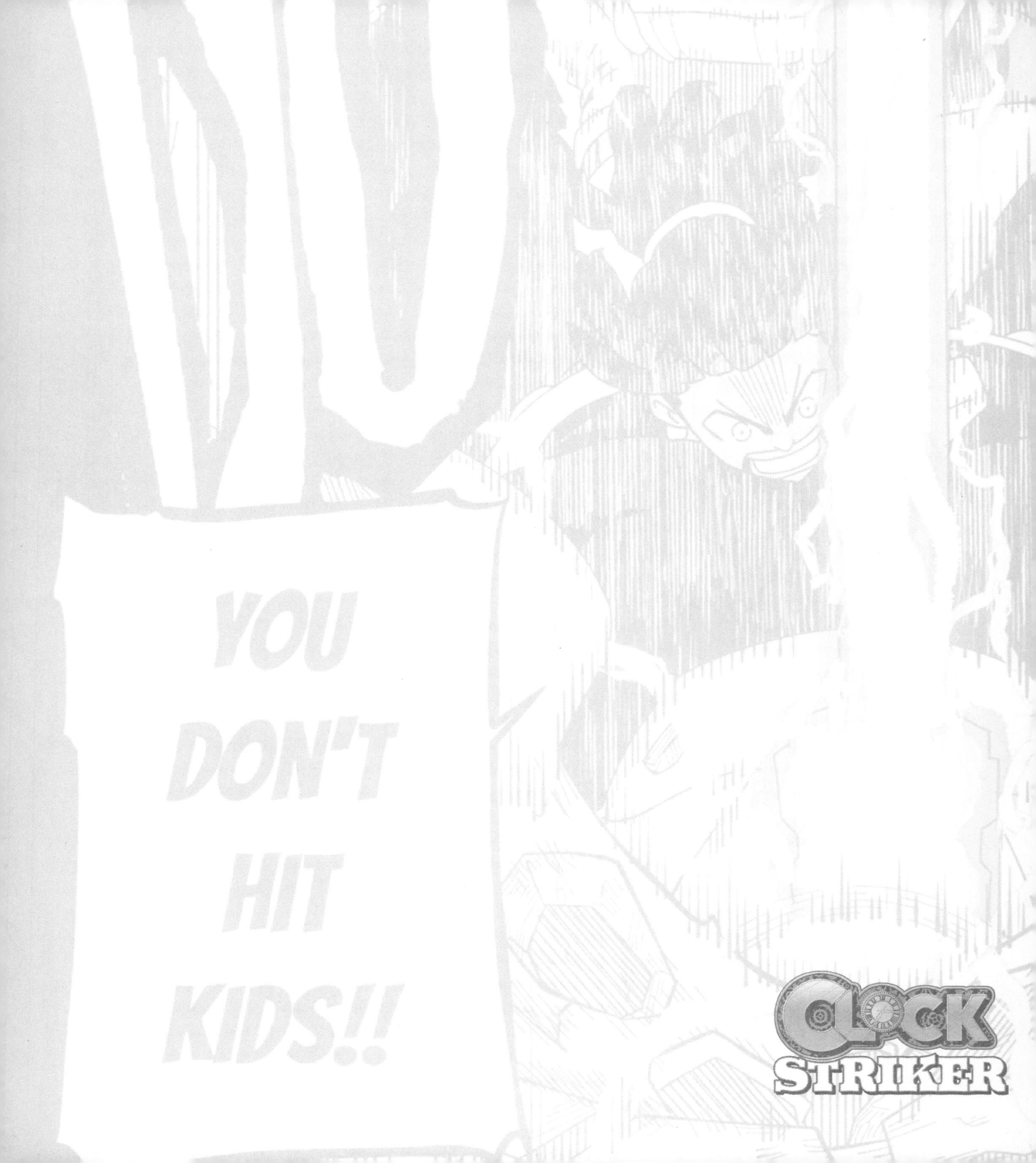
YOU DON'T HIT KIDS!!
CLOCK STRIKER

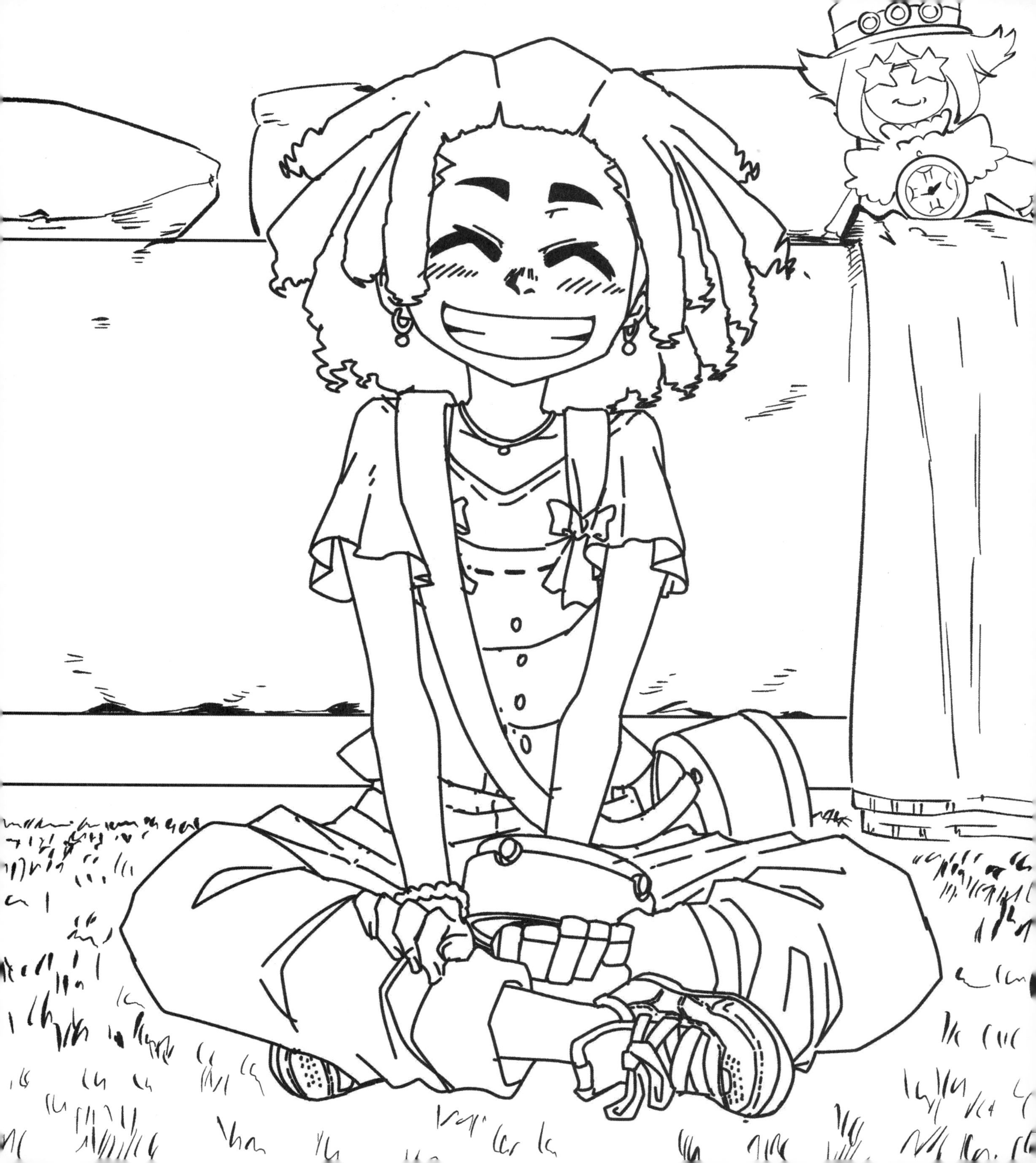

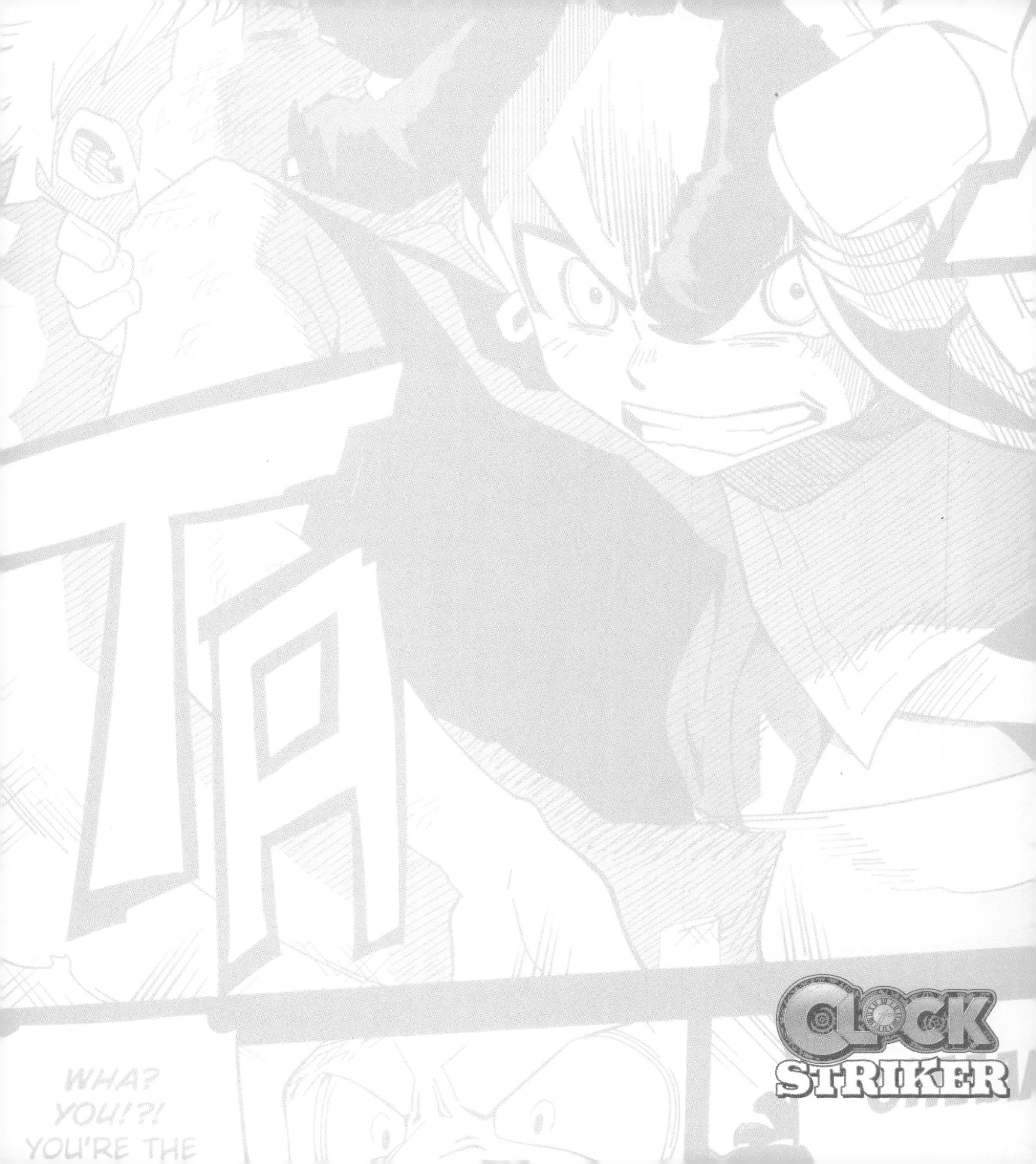
CLOCK STRIKER
WHA?
YOU!?!
YOU'RE THE

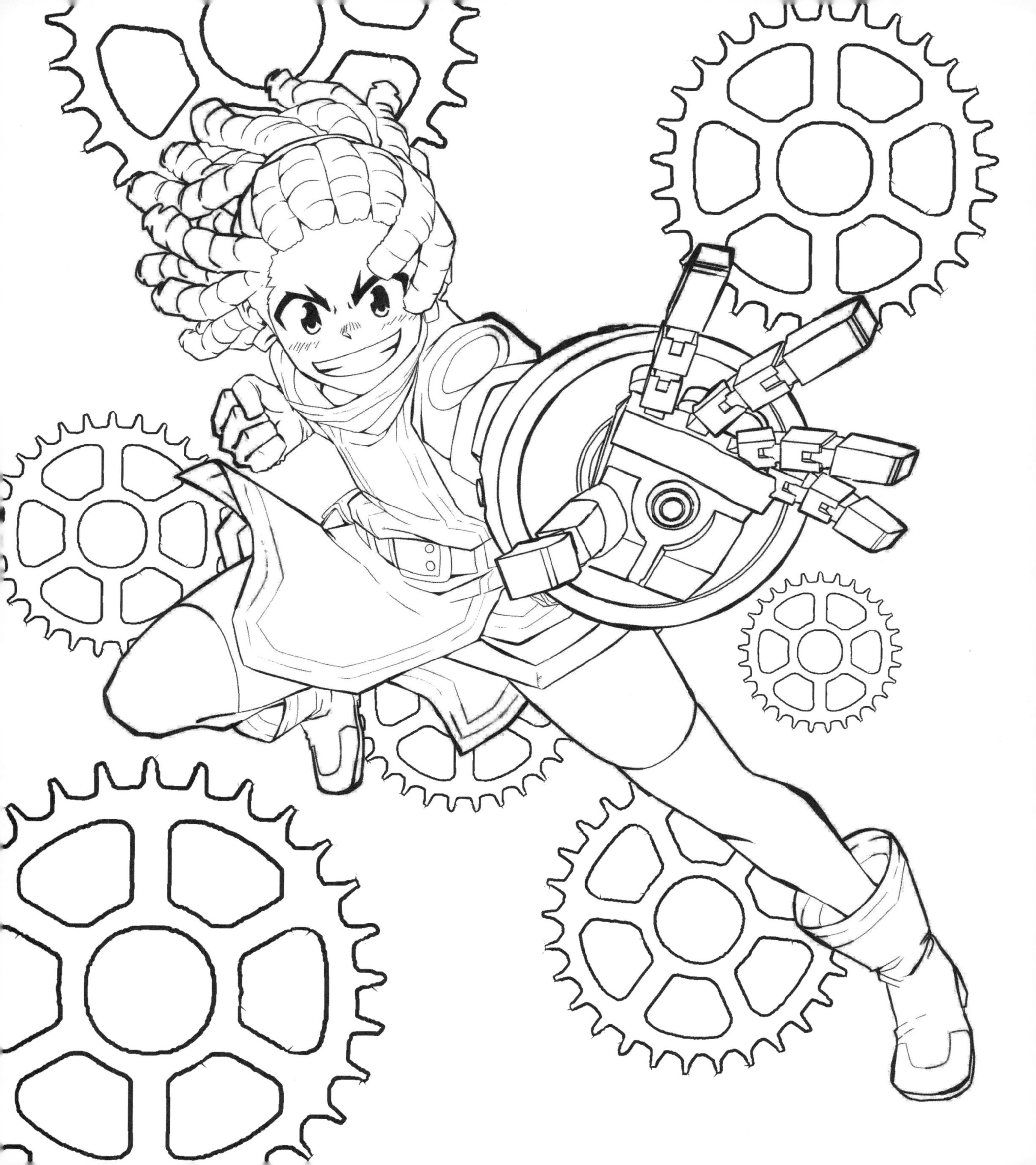

CLOCK STRIKER

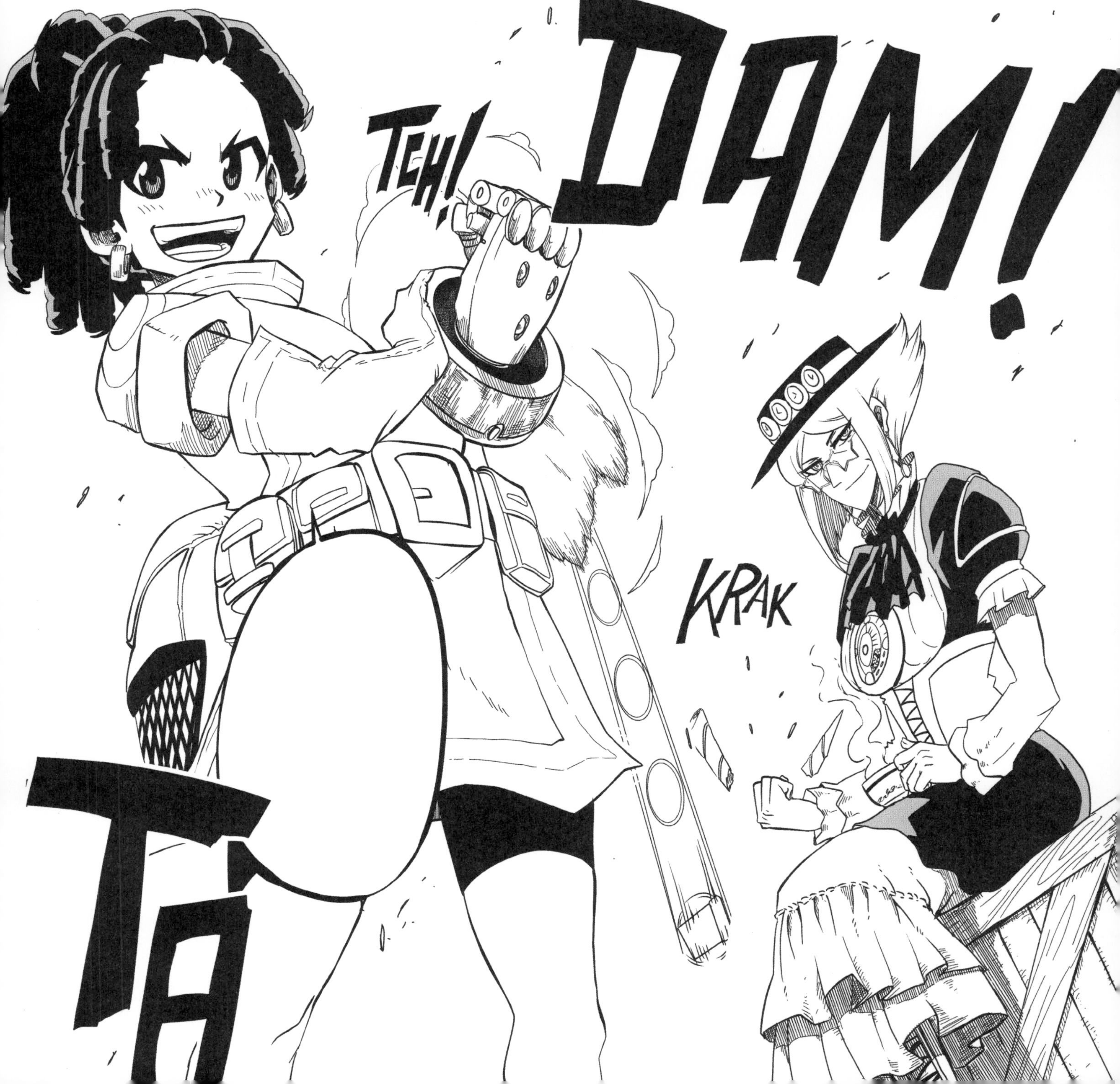
TCH!
DAM!
KRAK
TA

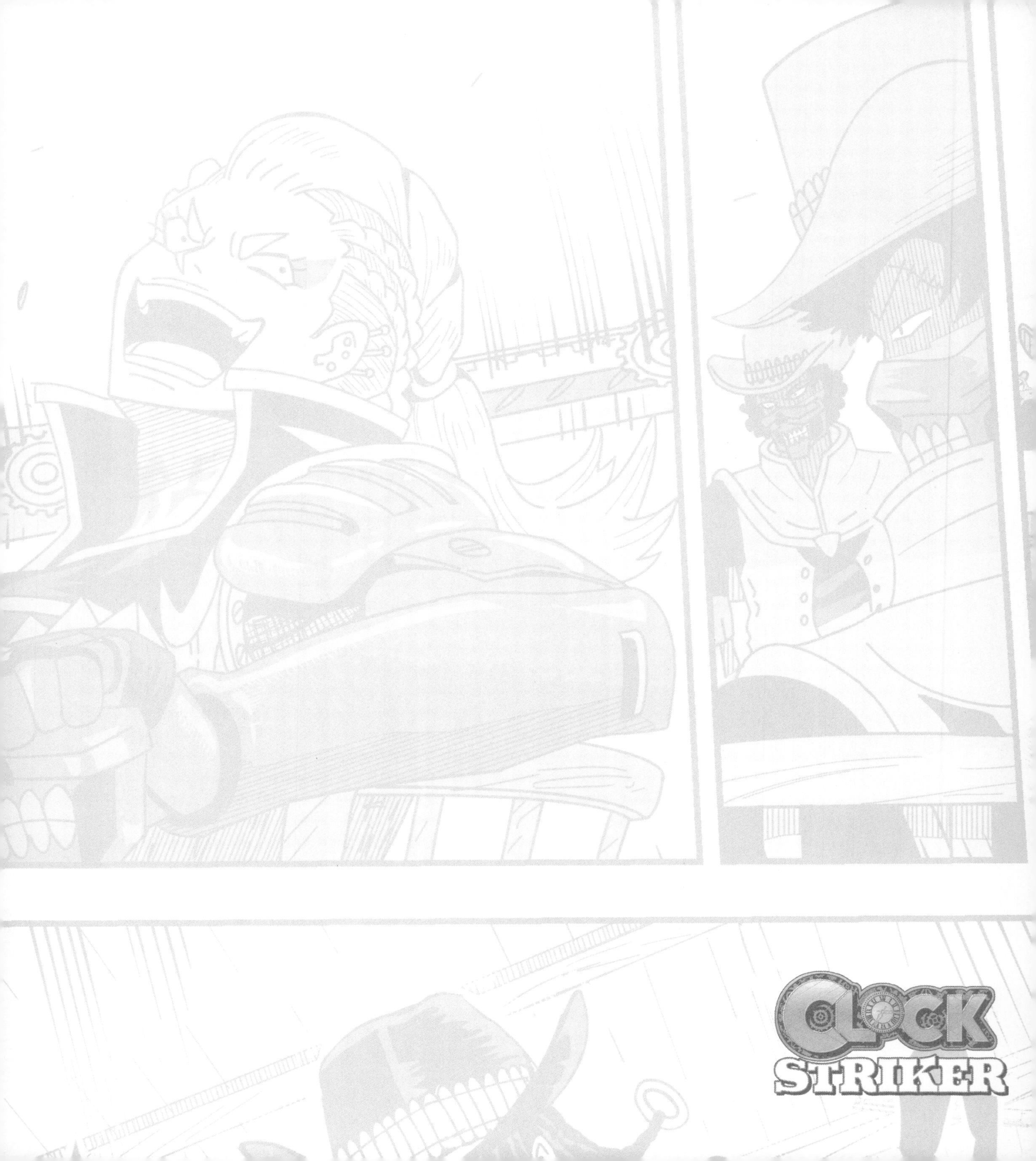
CLOCK
STRIKER

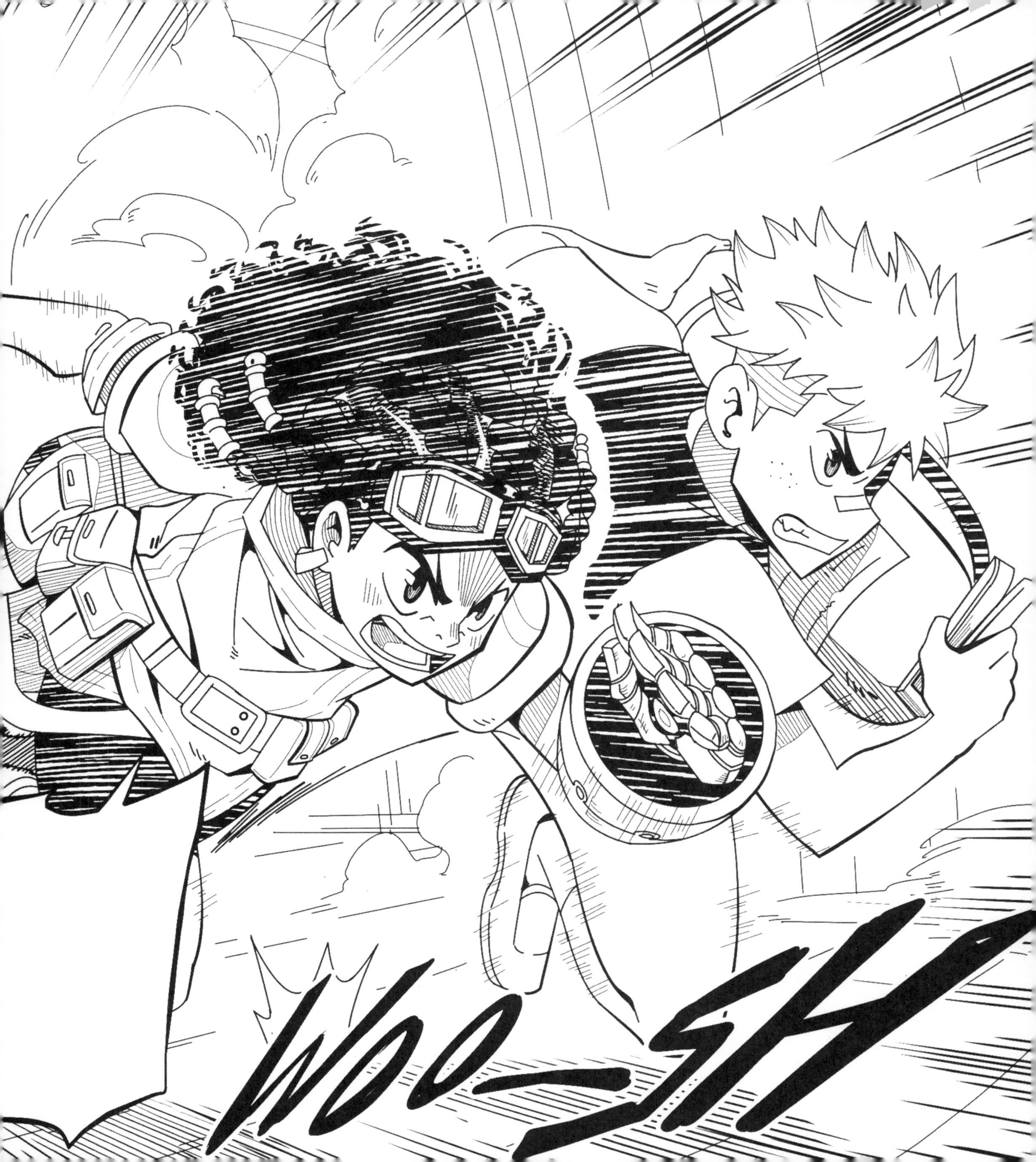
WOOSH

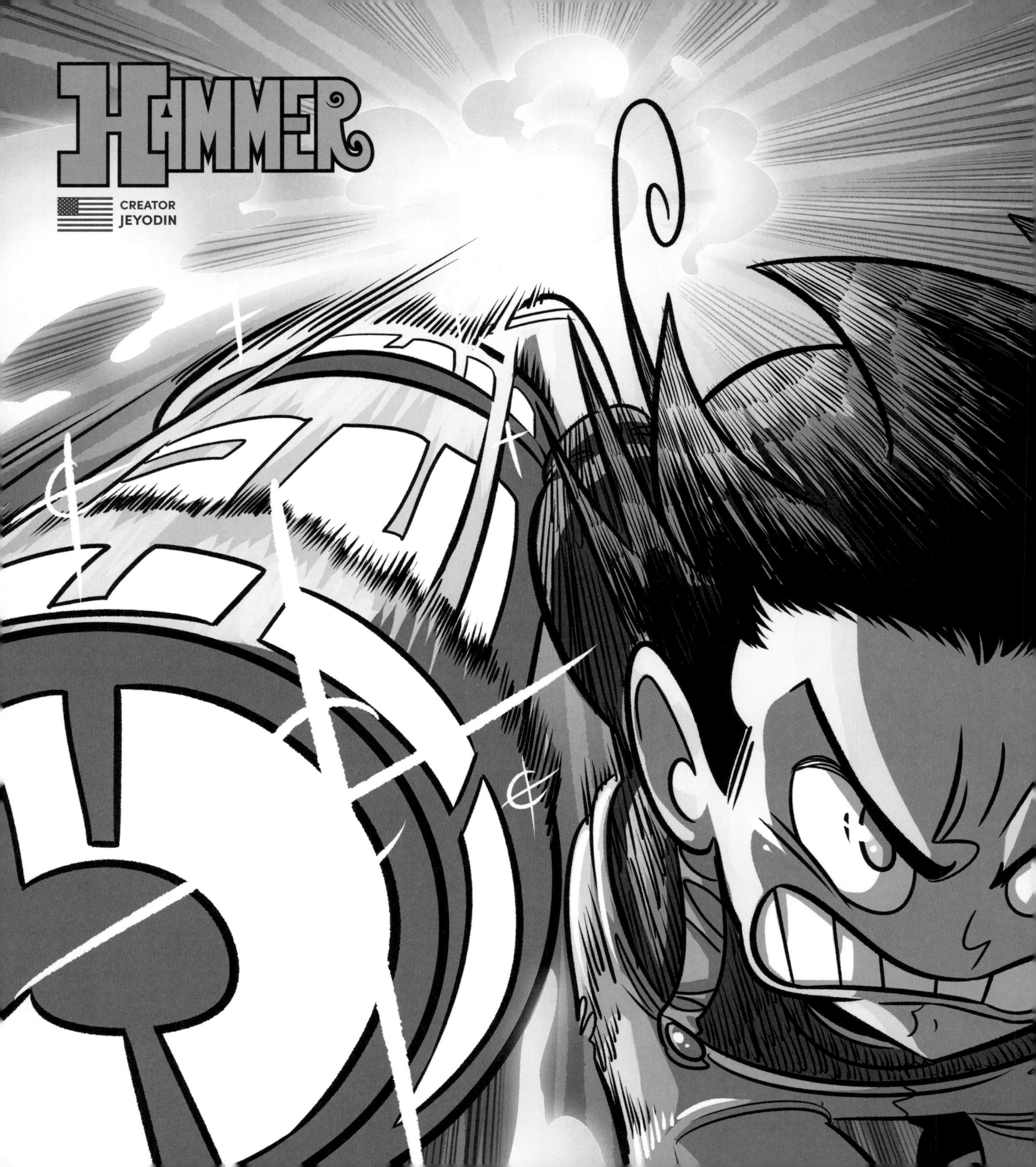
HAMMER
CREATOR
JEYODIN

STUD

NAME: STUD NAIL HAMMER

HEIGHT: 5'1"

SERIES: HAMMER

BIO: Overly optimistic and simple, Stud is a weird kid who talks to himself. After turning thirteen, Stud discovered his abnormal ability, which allows him to turn any part of his body into a hammer or a nail. As a "Metal Fighter," he can also turn his entire body into metal.

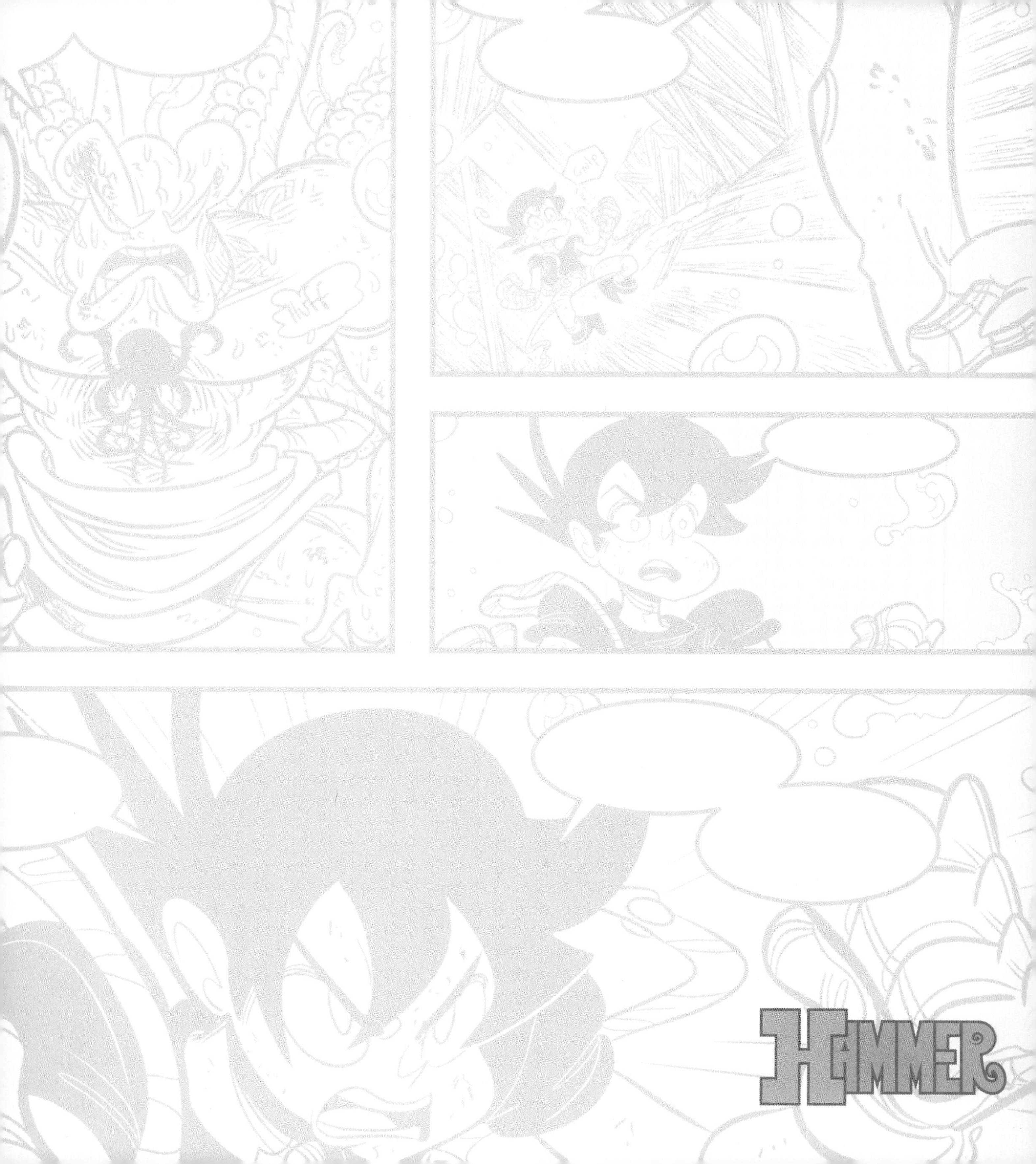
Huff
Gulp

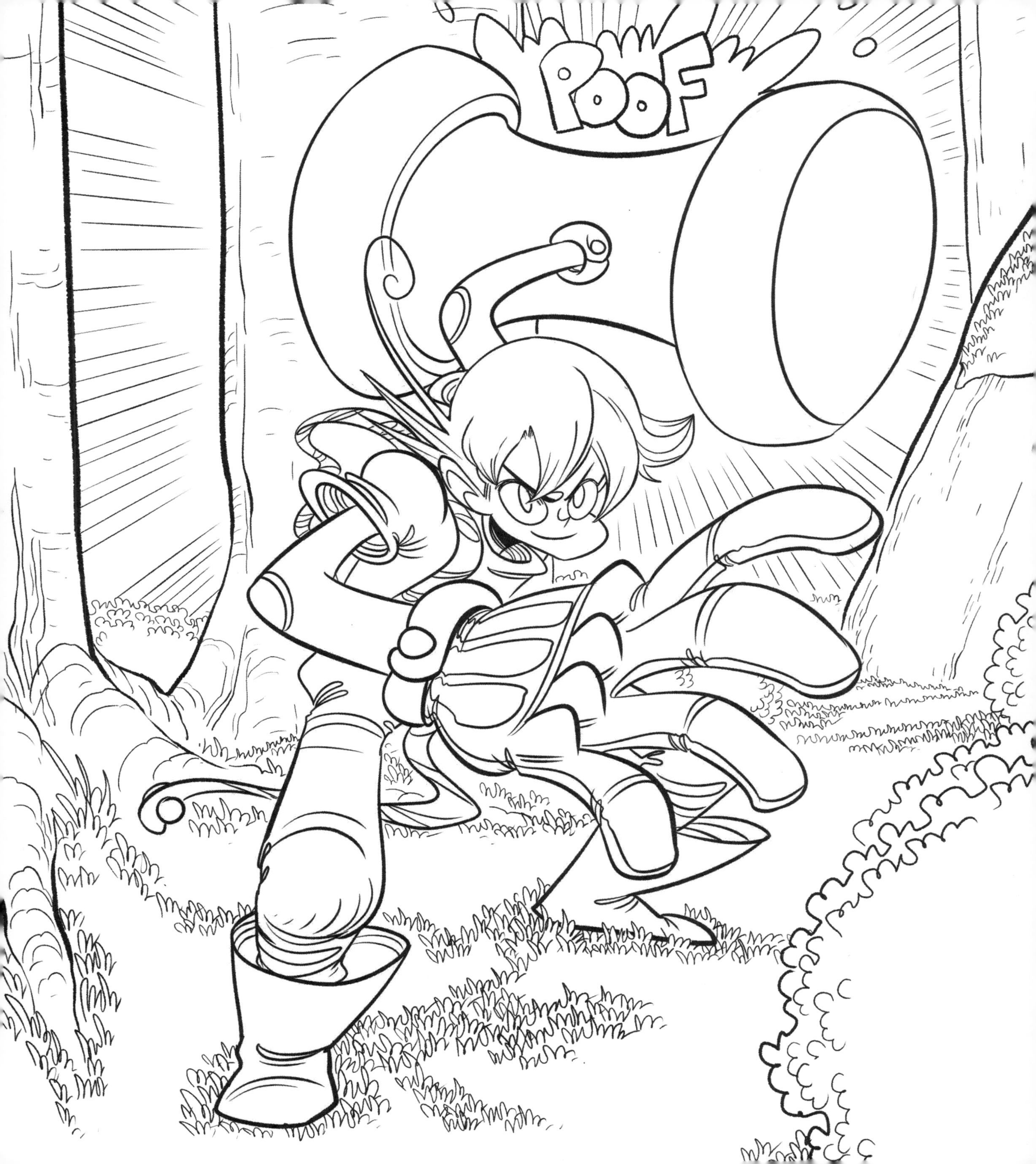
POOF

HAMMER

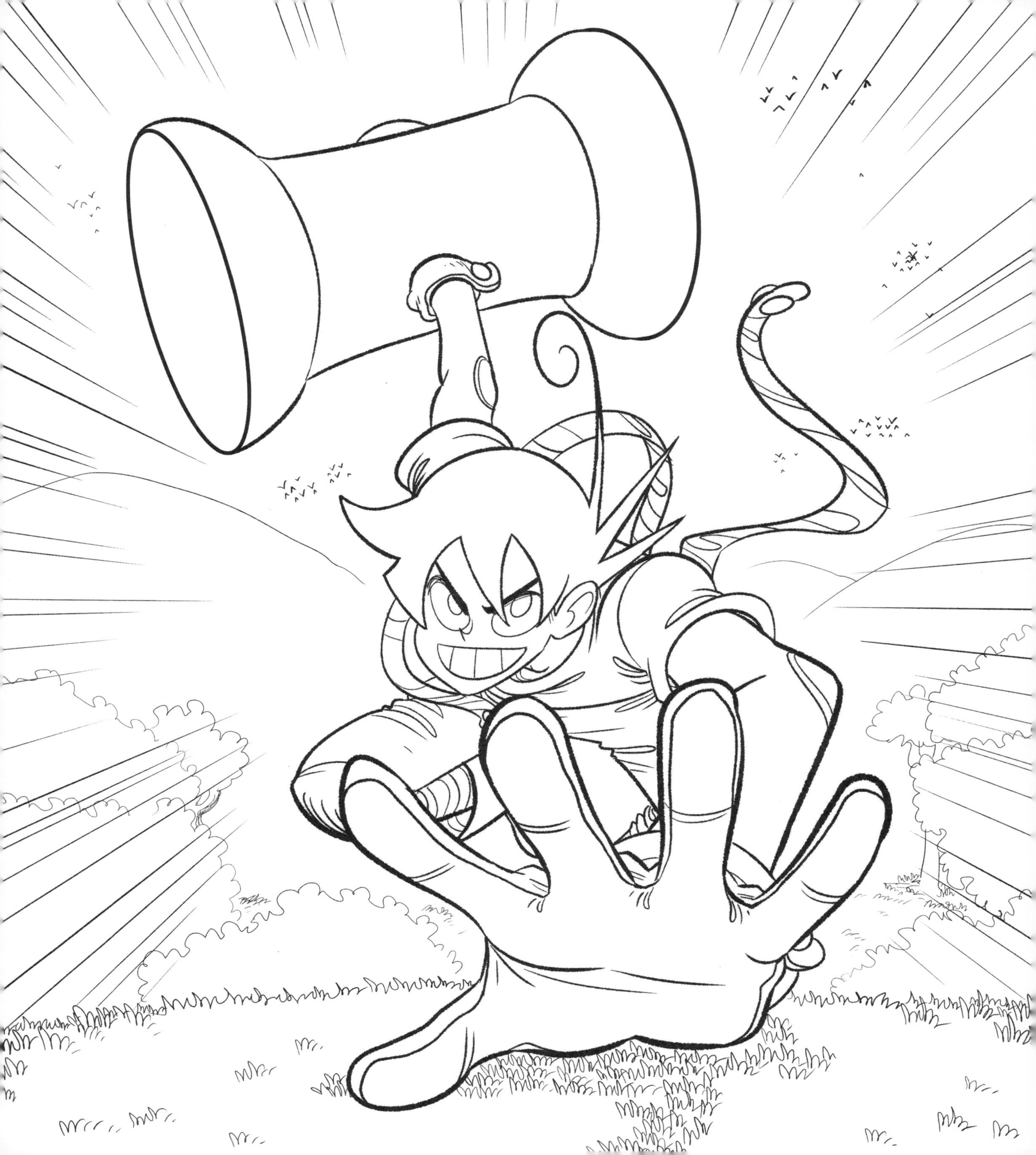

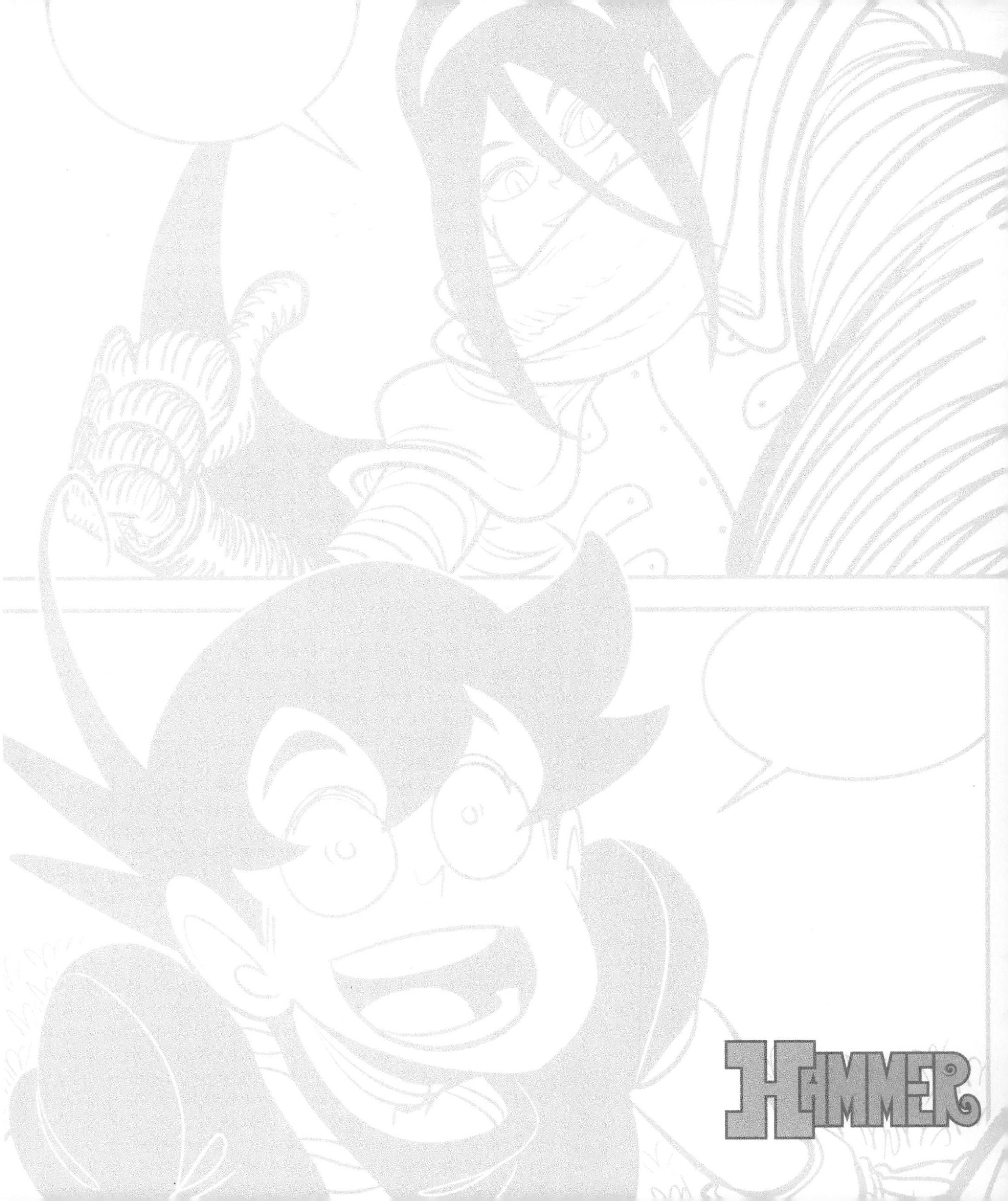

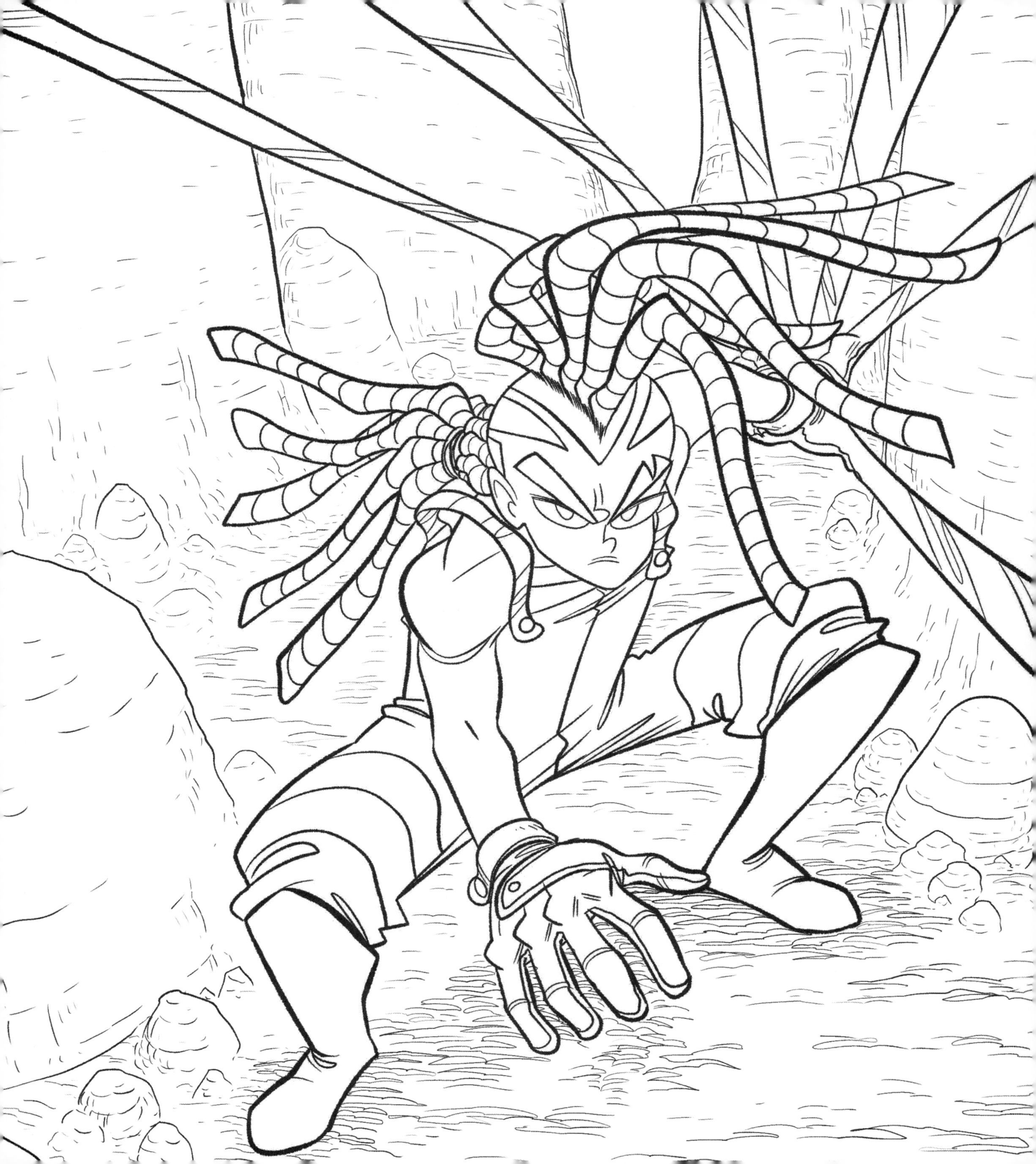

HAMMER®

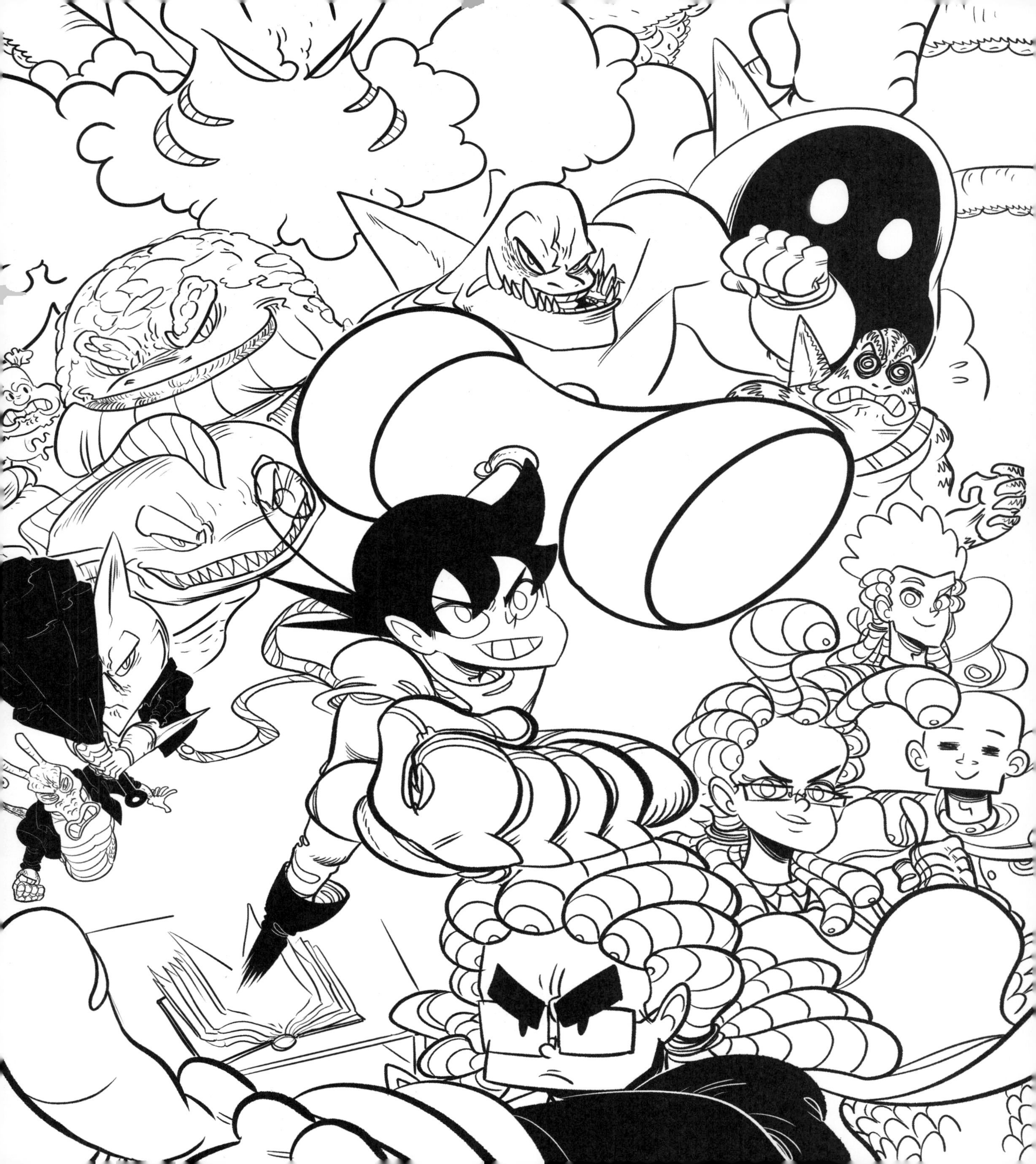

SOUL BEAT

CREATOR
MORGANNE WALKER

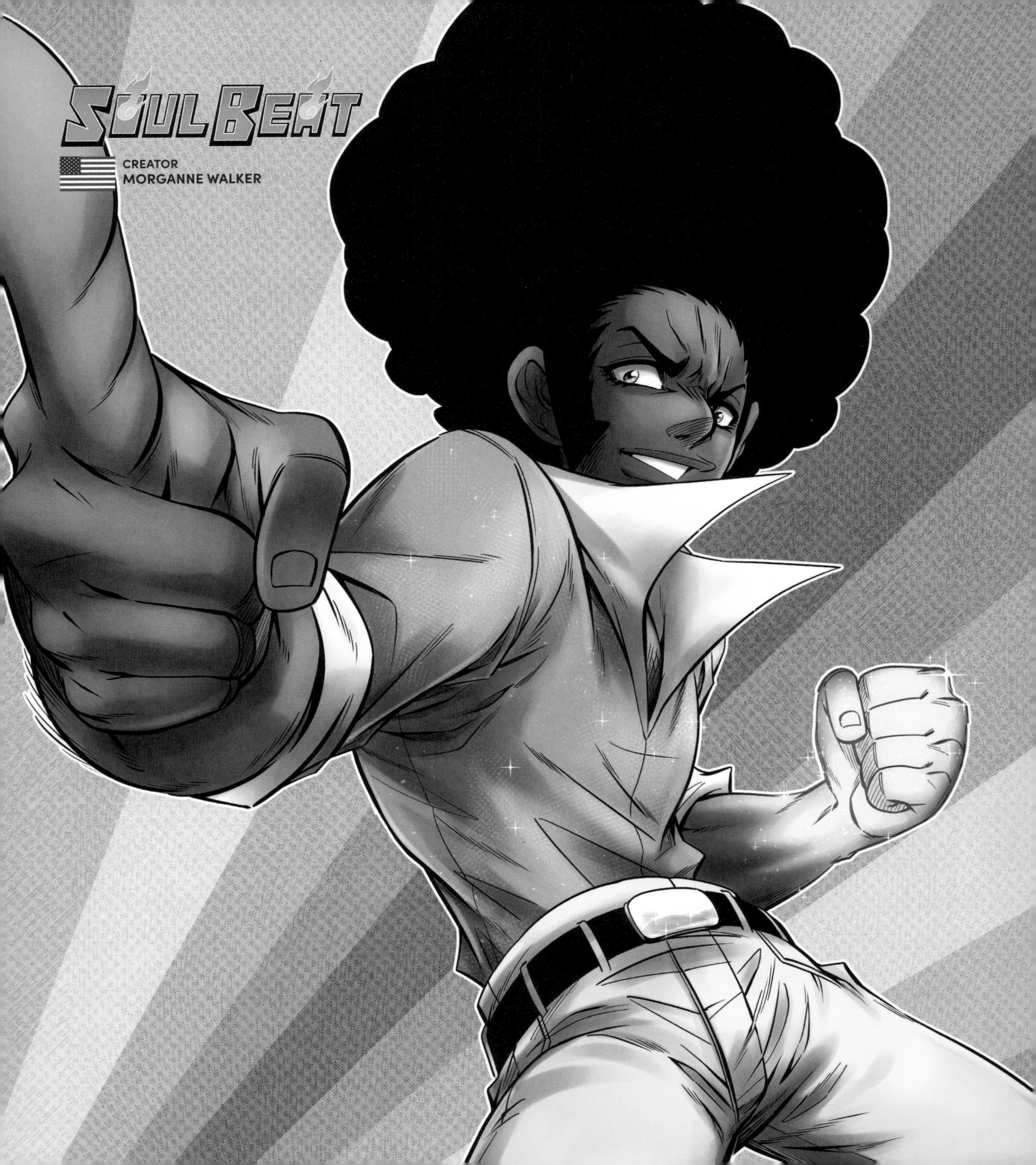

DANTE

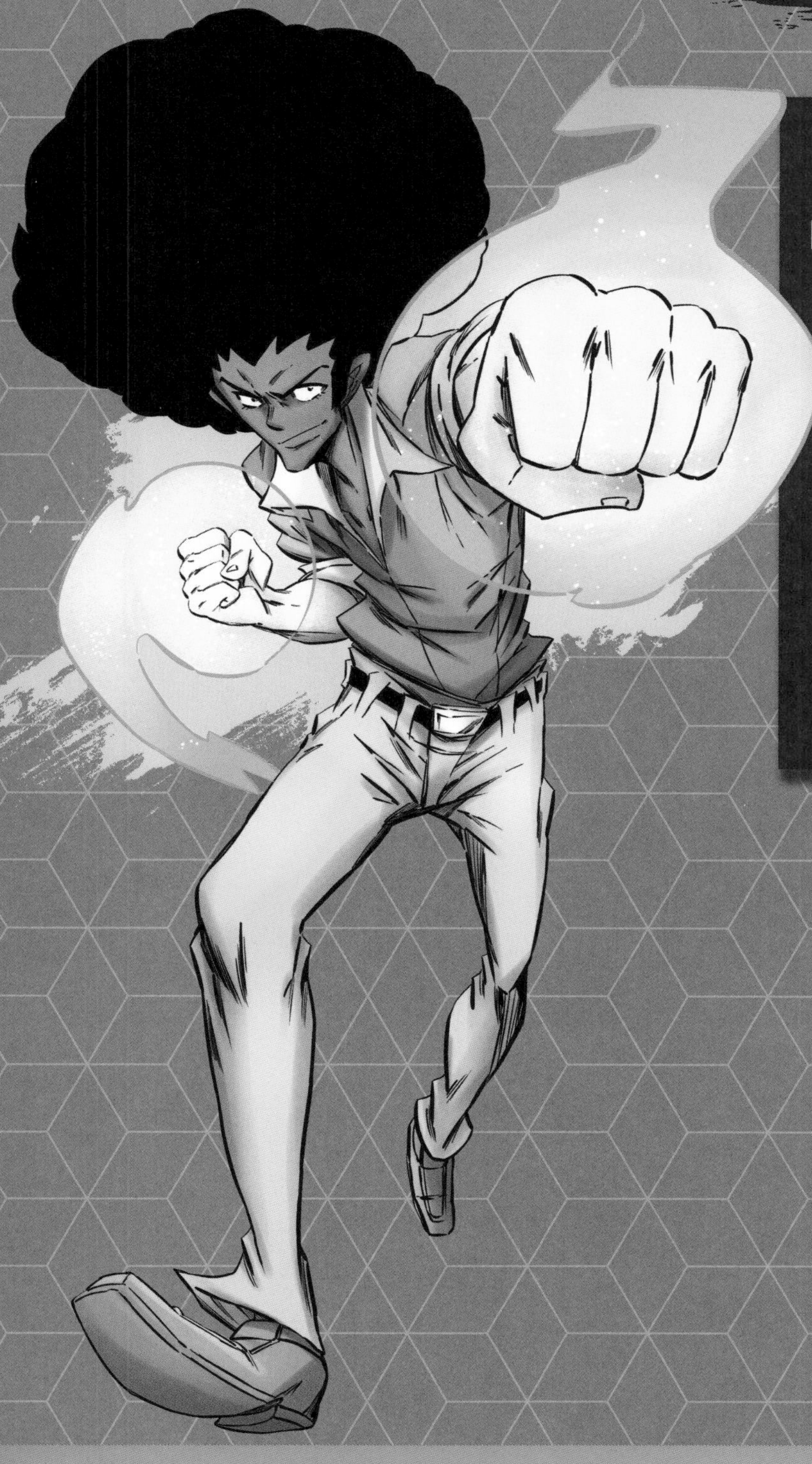

NAME: DANTE ALFONSE

HEIGHT: 6'0"

SERIES: SOUL BEAT

BIO: Most of his life, Dante spent his days chasing many desires and causing trouble. Despite living alone in the quiet town of Fairhaven, he enjoys indulging in the city life and all of its guilty pleasures.

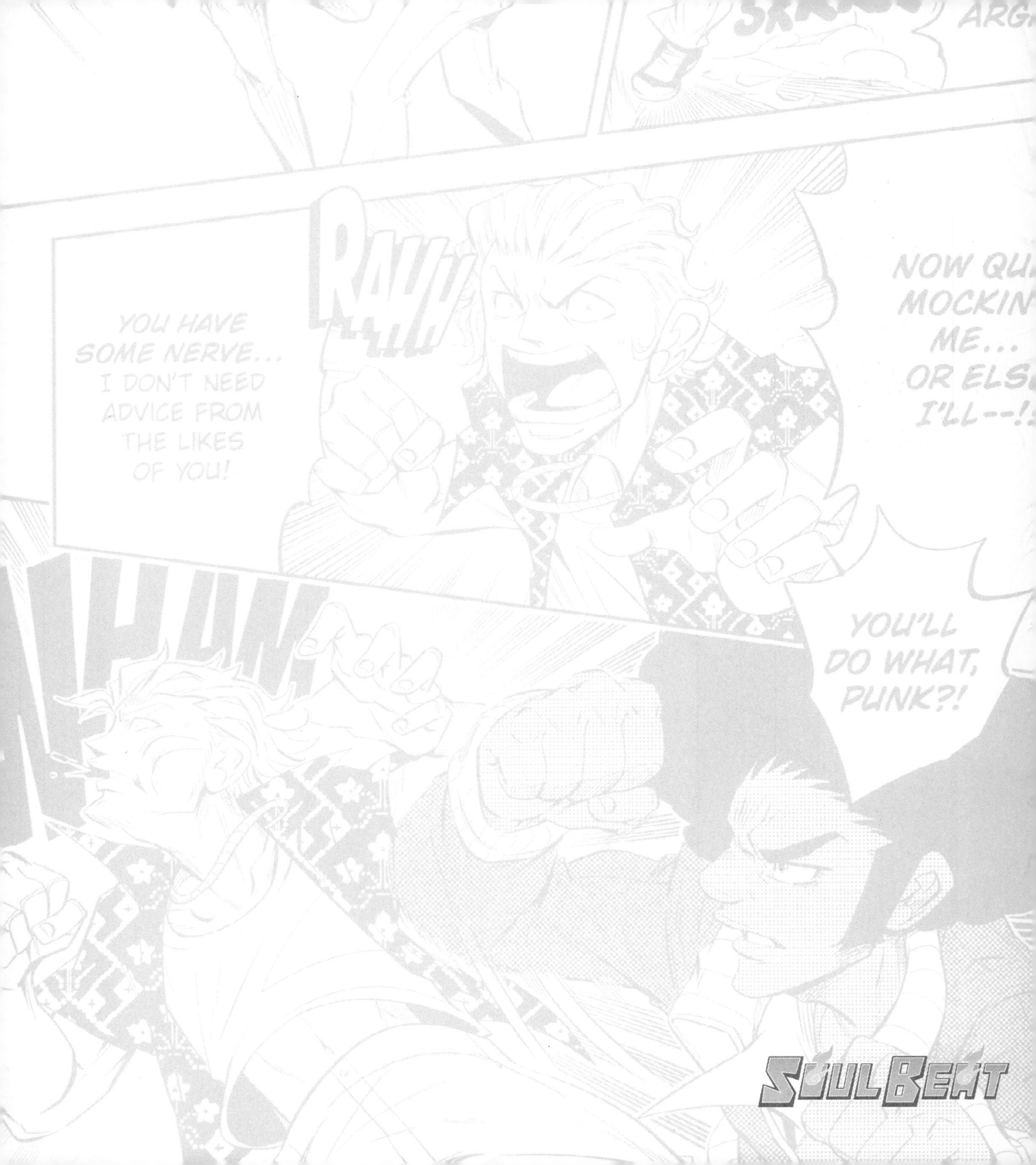
RAHH
YOU HAVE SOME NERVE... I DON'T NEED ADVICE FROM THE LIKES OF YOU!
NOW QU MOCKIN ME... OR ELS I'LL--!
YOU'LL DO WHAT, PUNK?!
SOUL BEAT

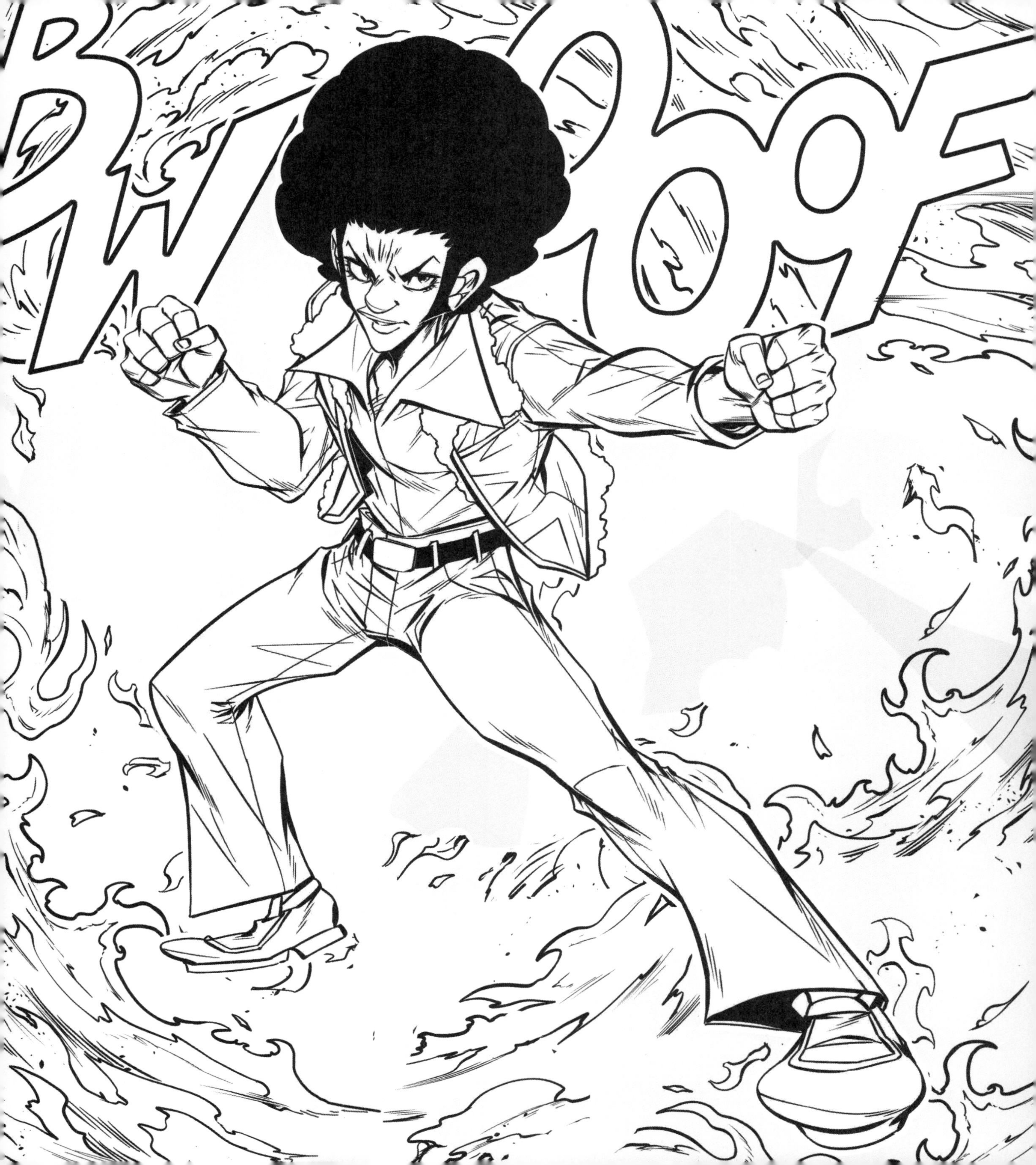
BWOOF

SOUL BEAT

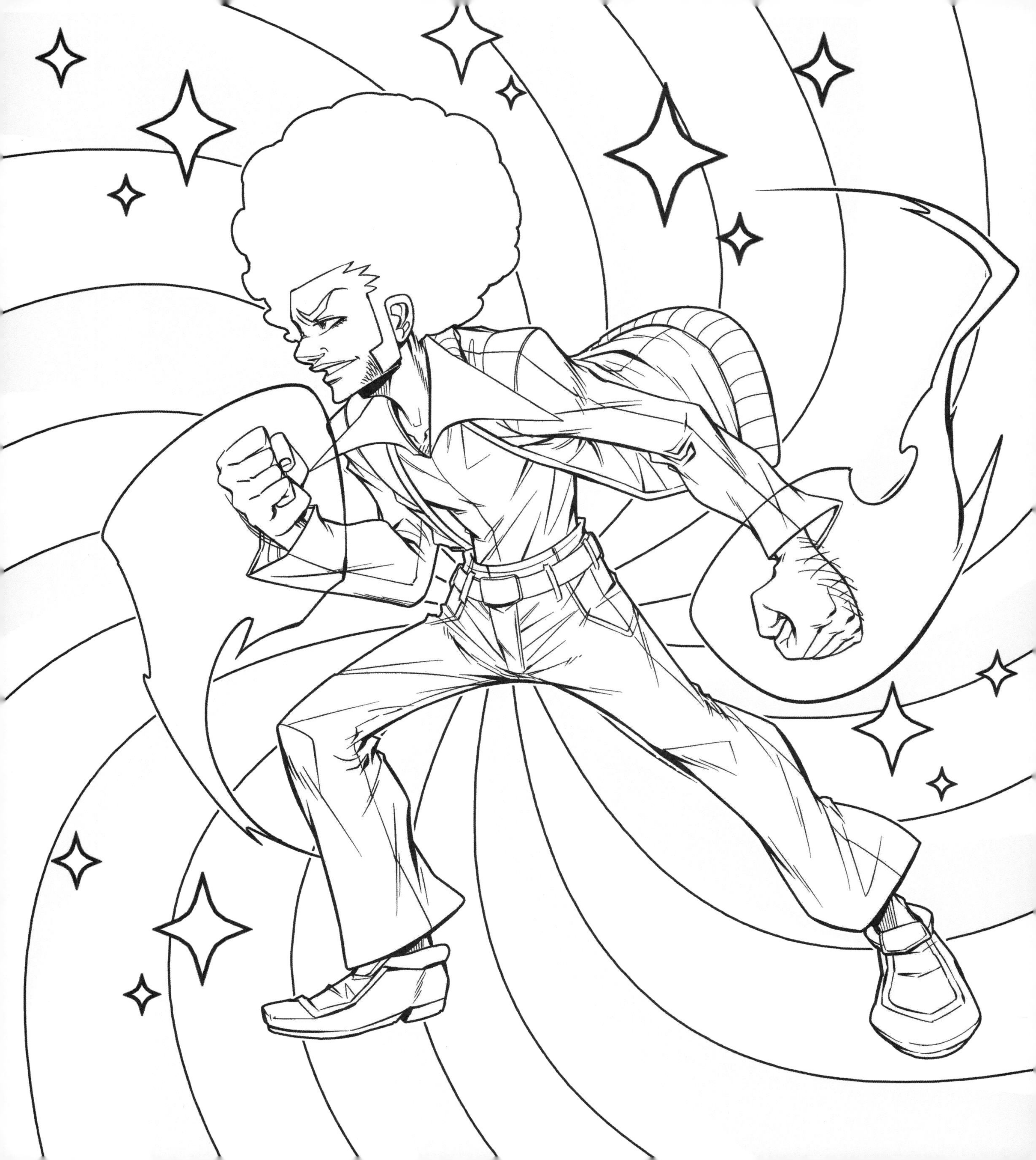

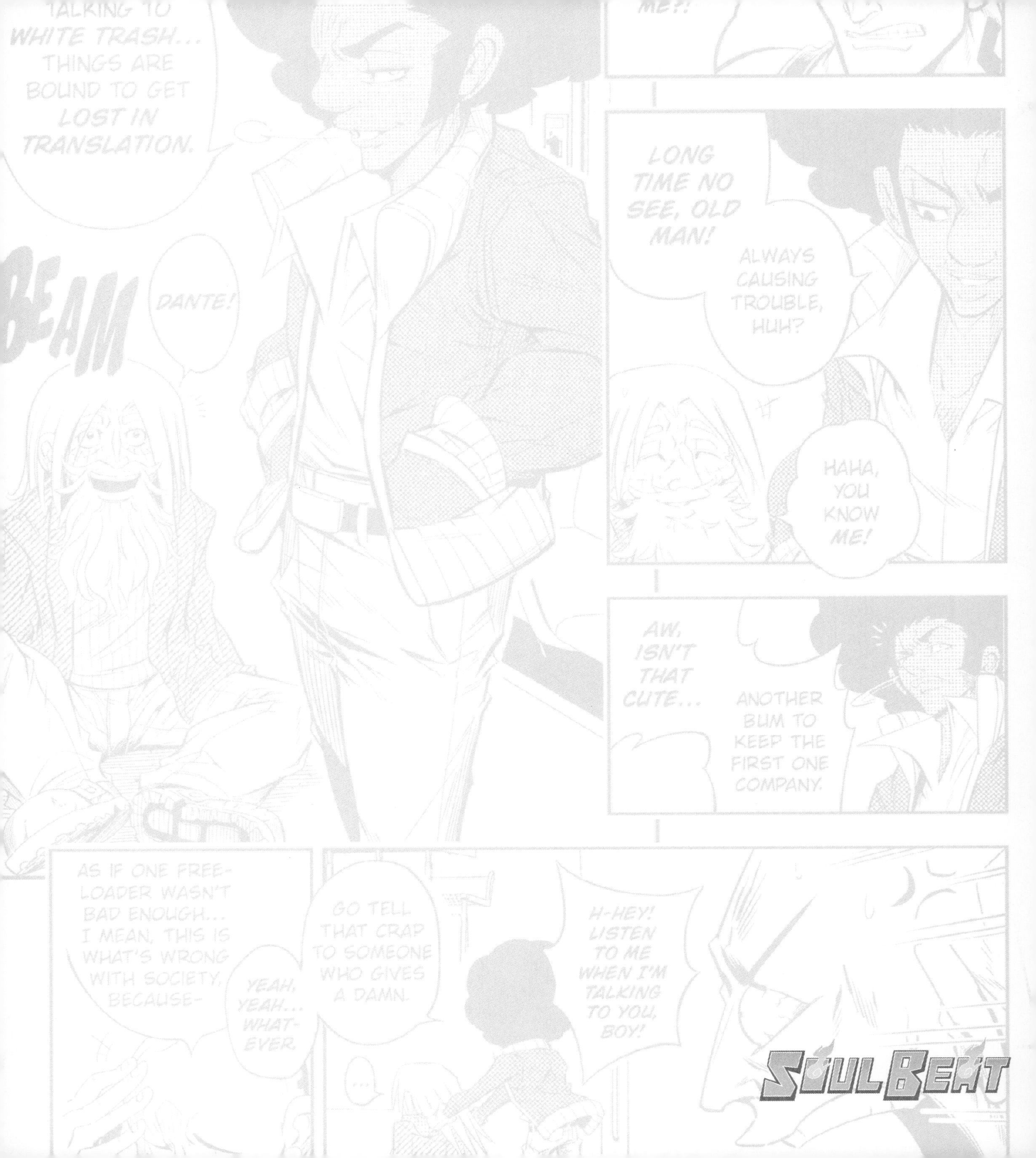
TALKING TO WHITE TRASH... THINGS ARE BOUND TO GET LOST IN TRANSLATION.
ME?!
BEAM
DANTE!
LONG TIME NO SEE, OLD MAN!
ALWAYS CAUSING TROUBLE, HUH?
HAHA, YOU KNOW ME!
AW, ISN'T THAT CUTE...
ANOTHER BUM TO KEEP THE FIRST ONE COMPANY.
AS IF ONE FREE-LOADER WASN'T BAD ENOUGH... I MEAN, THIS IS WHAT'S WRONG WITH SOCIETY, BECAUSE-
YEAH, YEAH... WHAT-EVER.
GO TELL THAT CRAP TO SOMEONE WHO GIVES A DAMN.
...
H-HEY! LISTEN TO ME WHEN I'M TALKING TO YOU, BOY!
SOUL BEAT

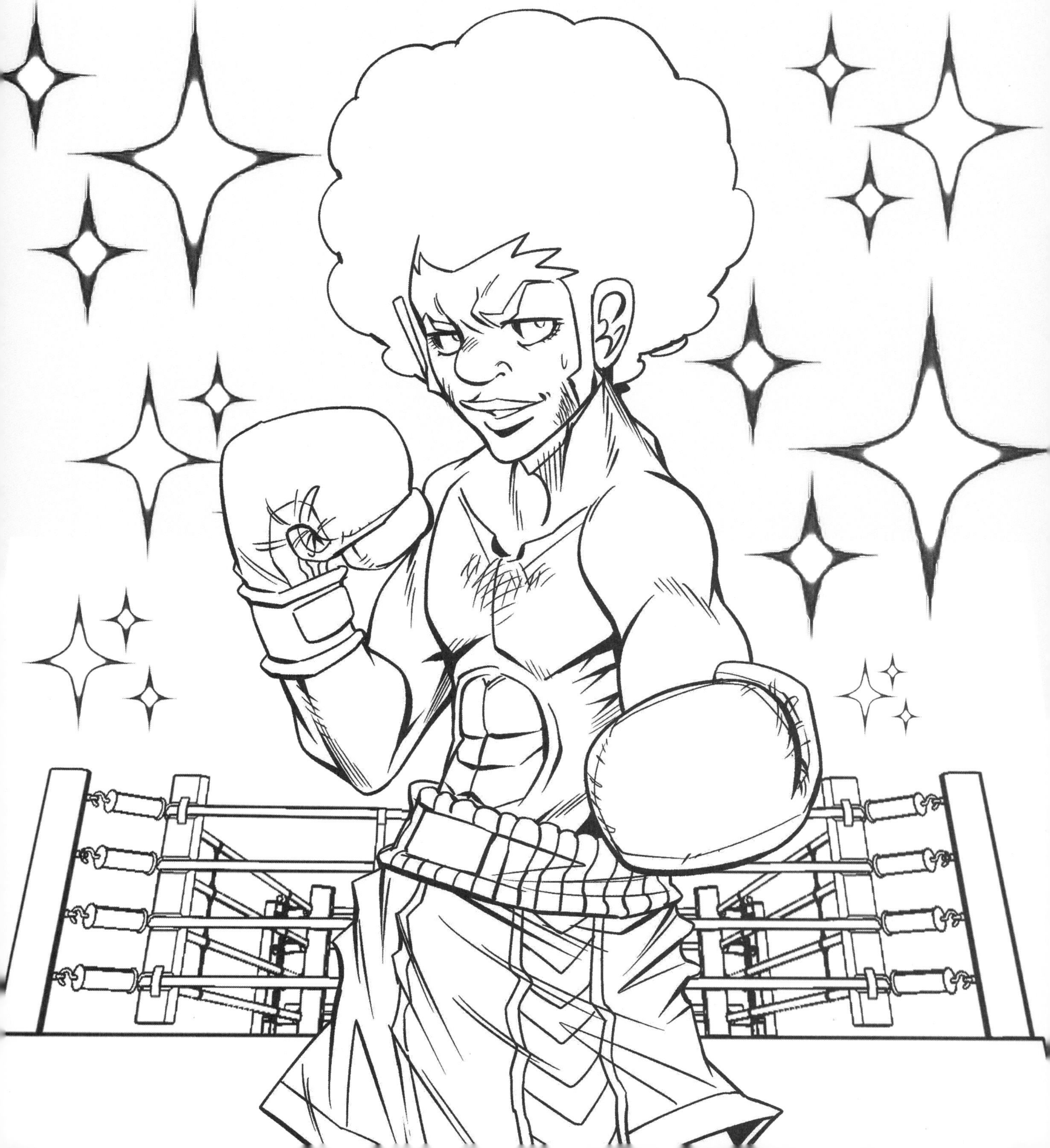

SOUL BEAT

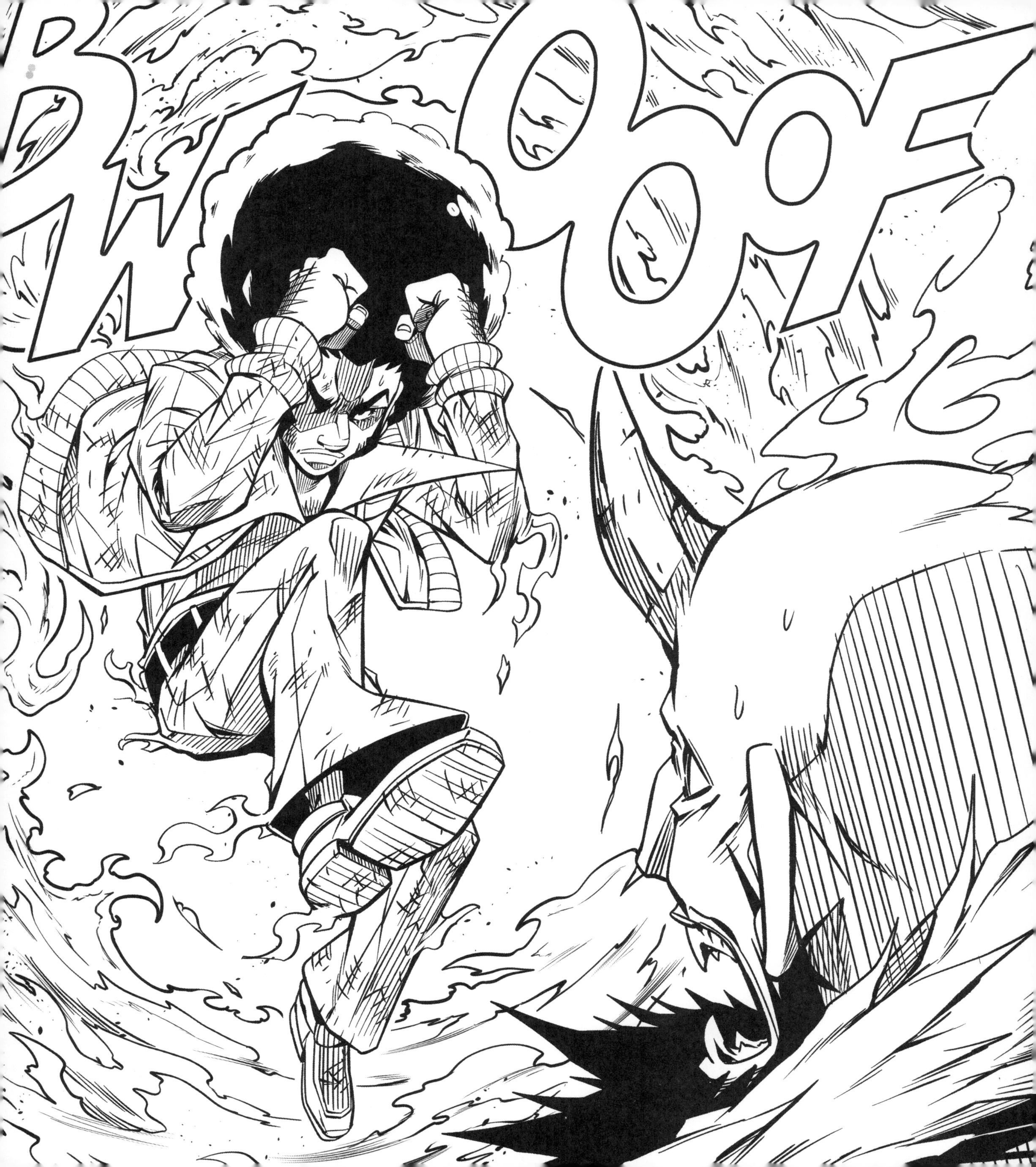
BWOOF

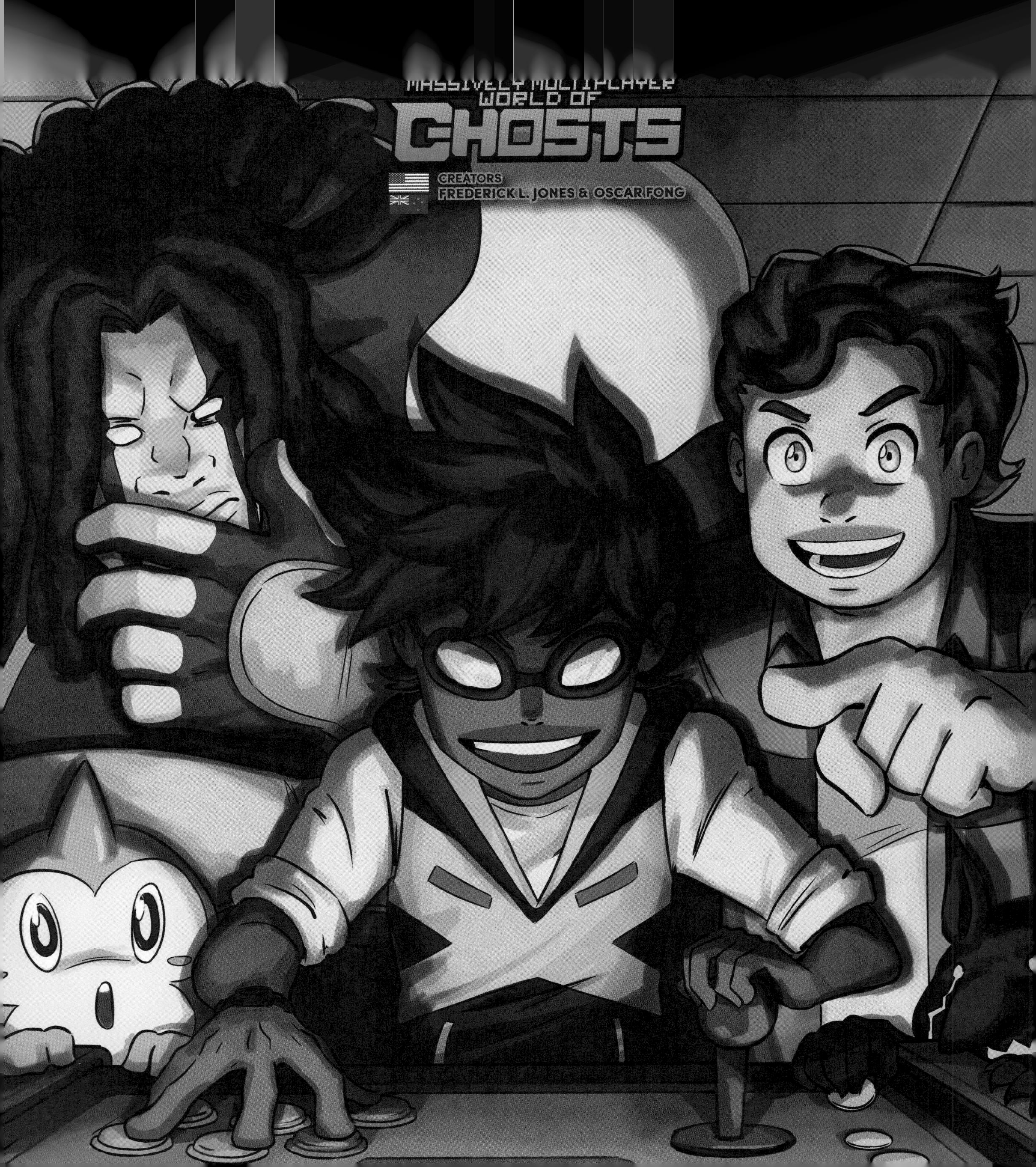
MASSIVELY MULTIPLAYER
WORLD OF
GHOSTS
CREATORS
FREDERICK L. JONES & OSCAR FONG

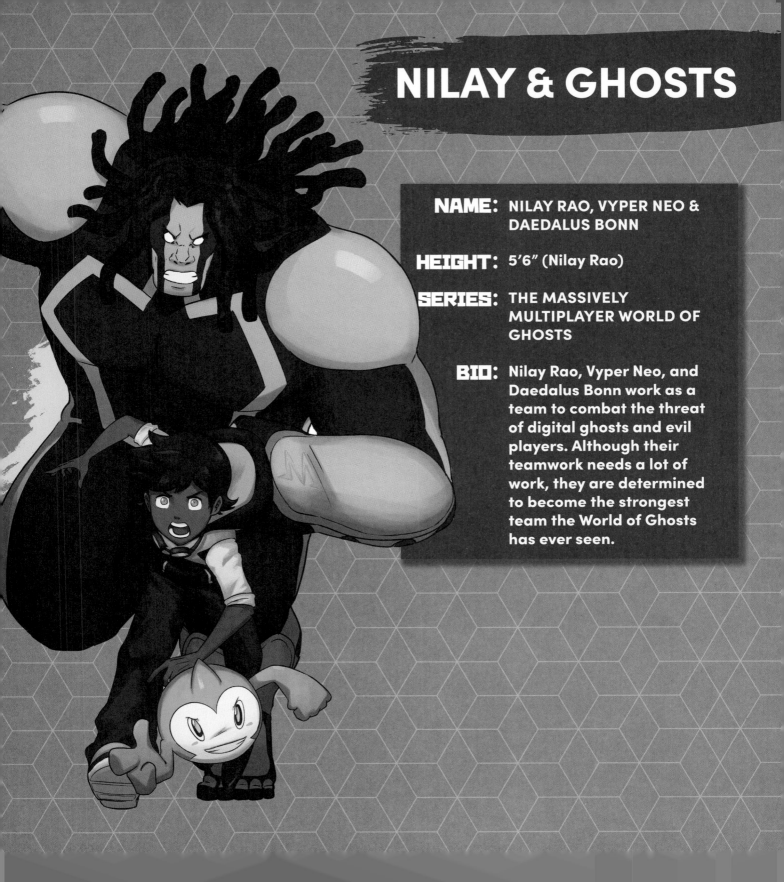

NILAY & GHOSTS

NAME: NILAY RAO, VYPER NEO & DAEDALUS BONN

HEIGHT: 5'6" (Nilay Rao)

SERIES: THE MASSIVELY MULTIPLAYER WORLD OF GHOSTS

BIO: Nilay Rao, Vyper Neo, and Daedalus Bonn work as a team to combat the threat of digital ghosts and evil players. Although their teamwork needs a lot of work, they are determined to become the strongest team the World of Ghosts has ever seen.

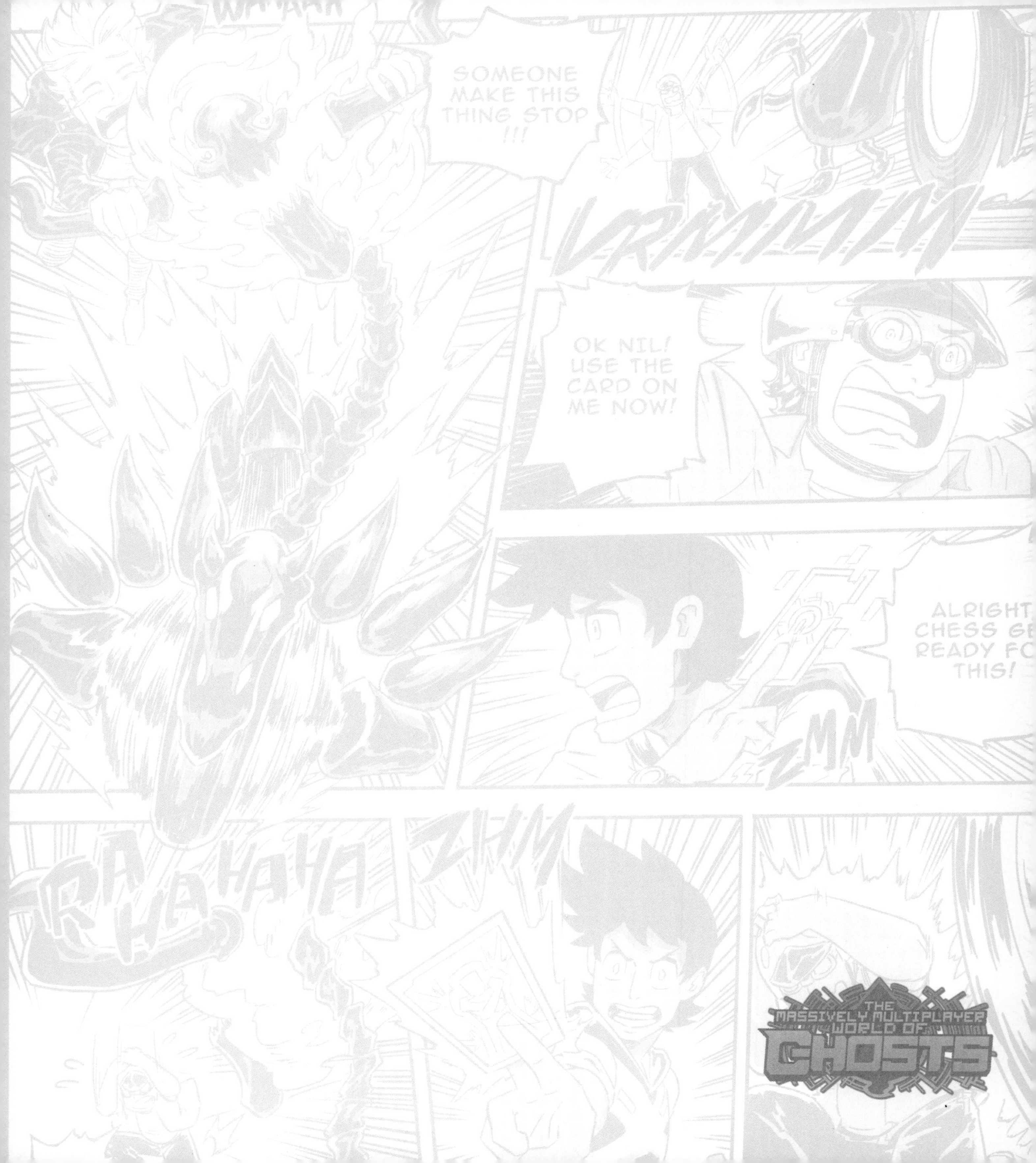
SOMEONE MAKE THIS THING STOP !!!
VRMMMM
OK NIL! USE THE CARD ON ME NOW!
ALRIGHT CHESS GE READY FO THIS!
ZMM
RAHAHAHA
ZHM
THE MASSIVELY MULTIPLAYER WORLD OF GHOSTS

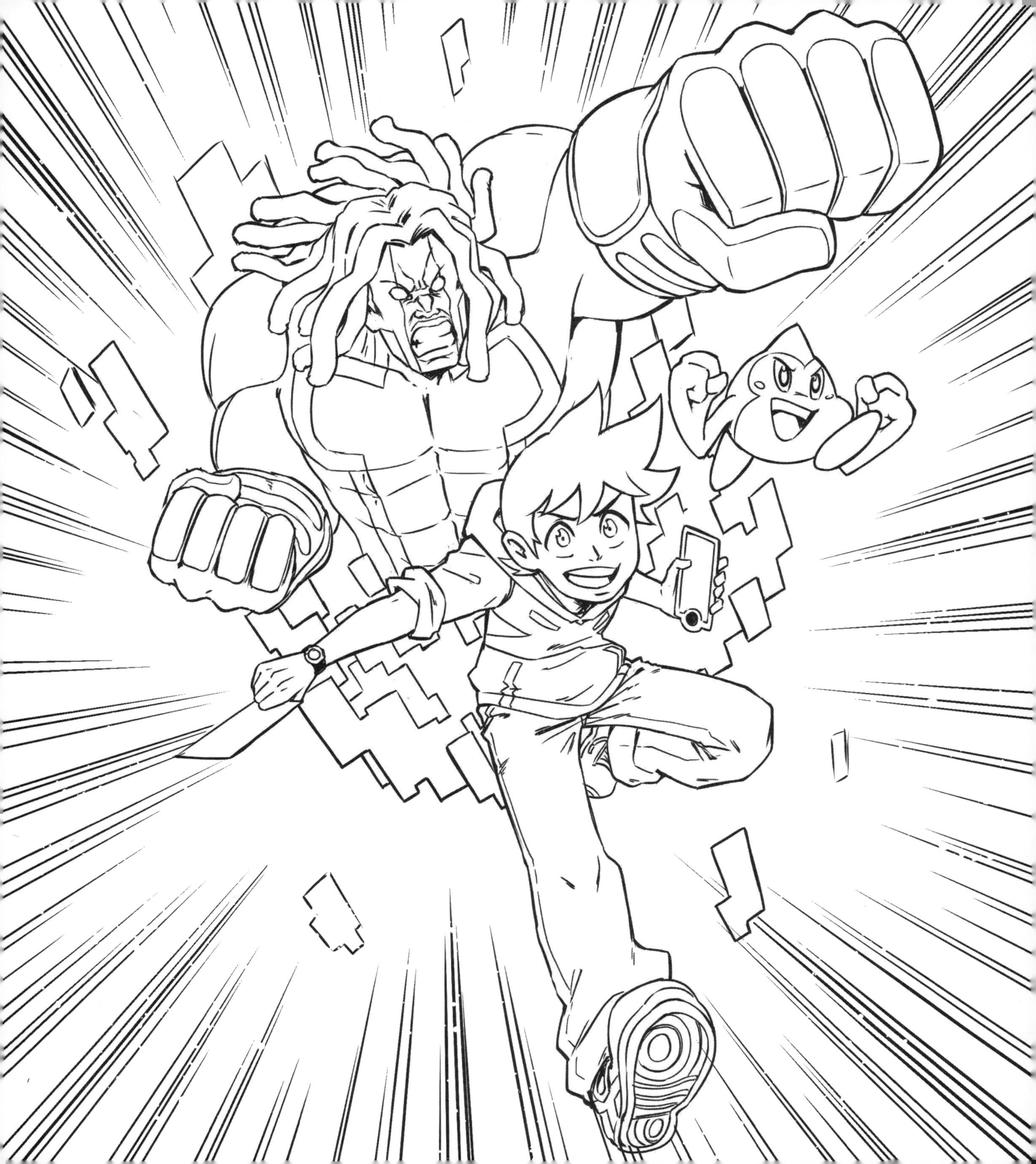

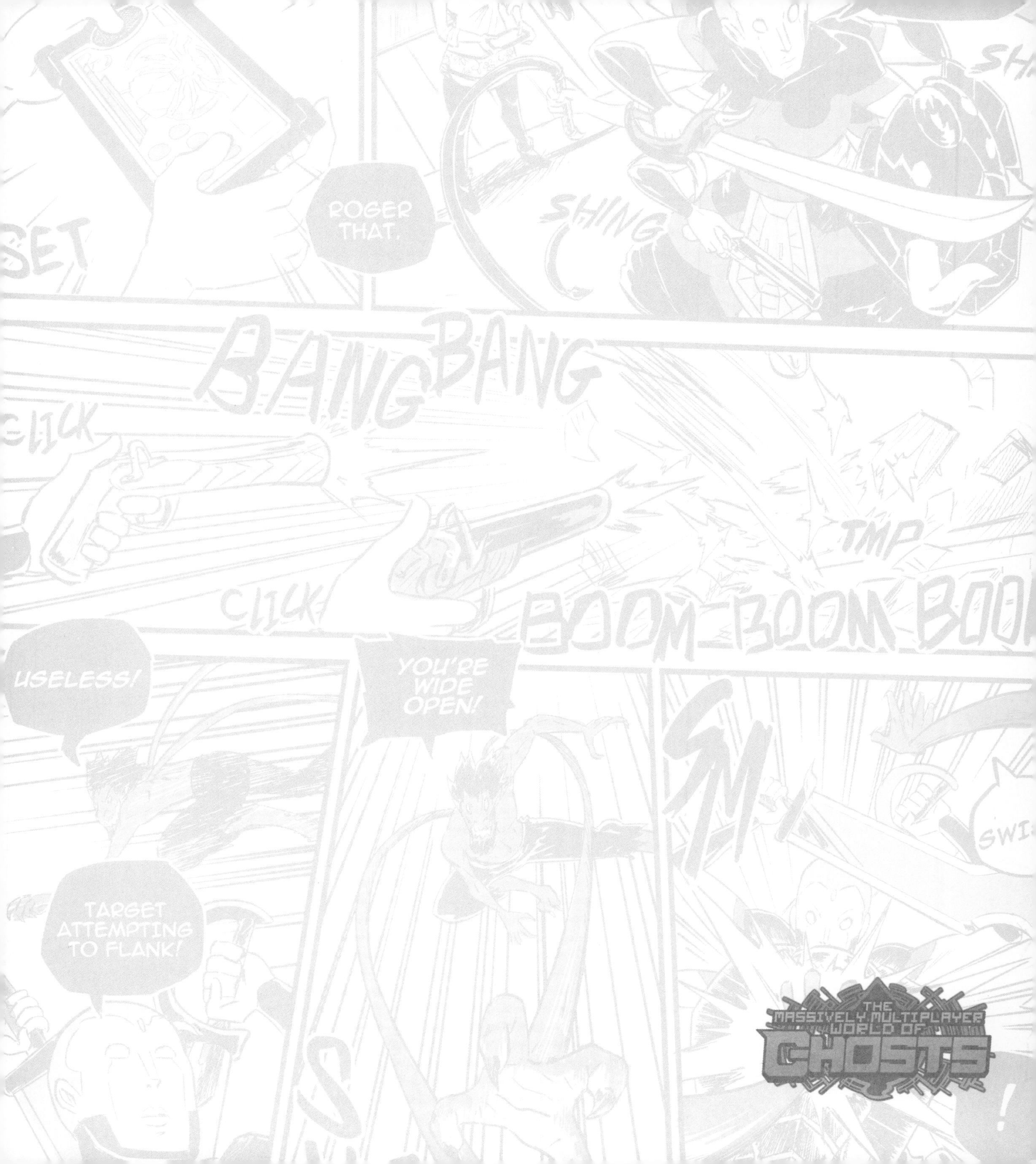
SET
ROGER THAT.
SHING
BANG BANG
CLICK
CLICK
TMP
USELESS!
YOU'RE WIDE OPEN!
TARGET ATTEMPTING TO FLANK!
THE MASSIVELY MULTIPLAYER WORLD OF GHOSTS

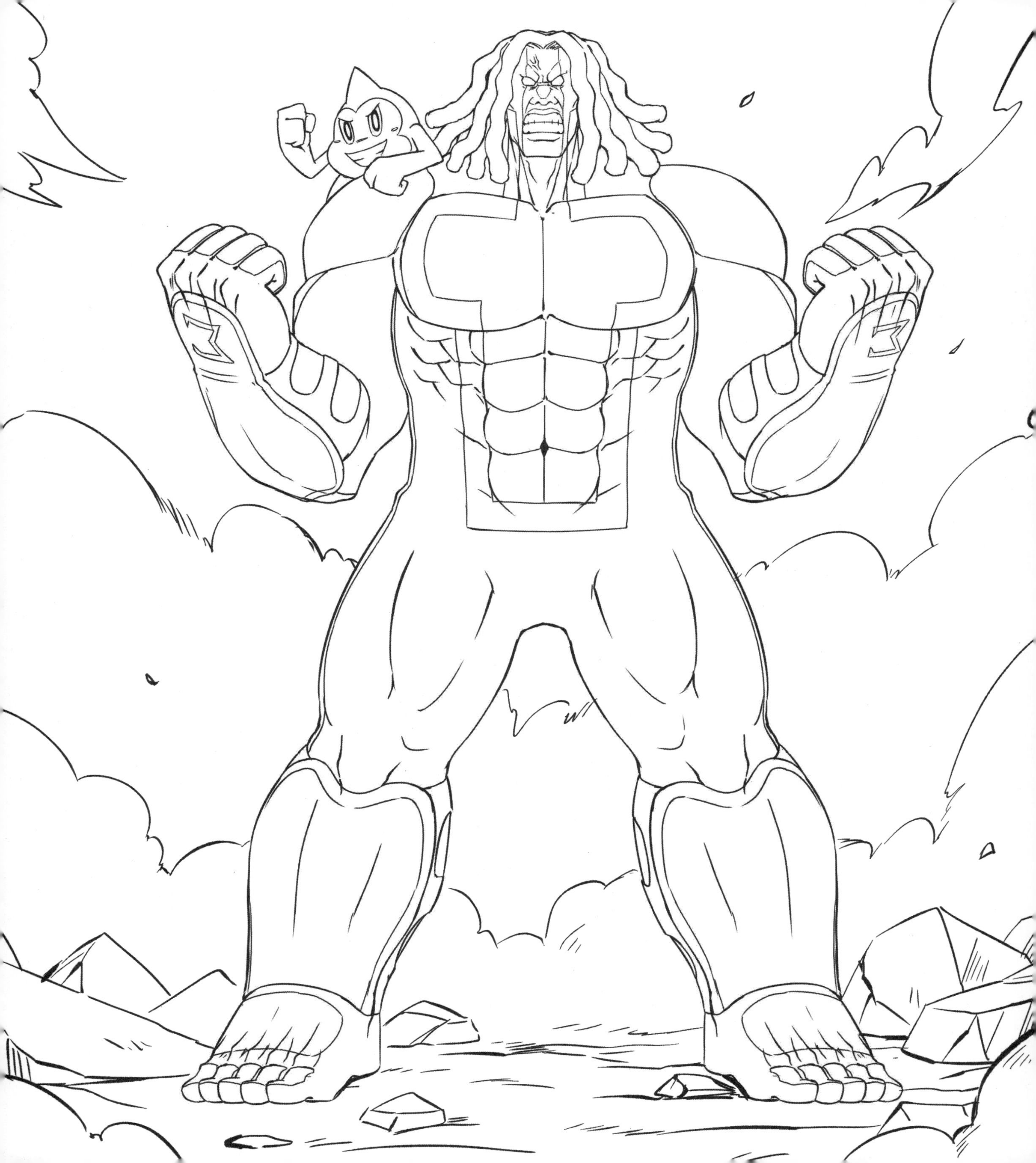

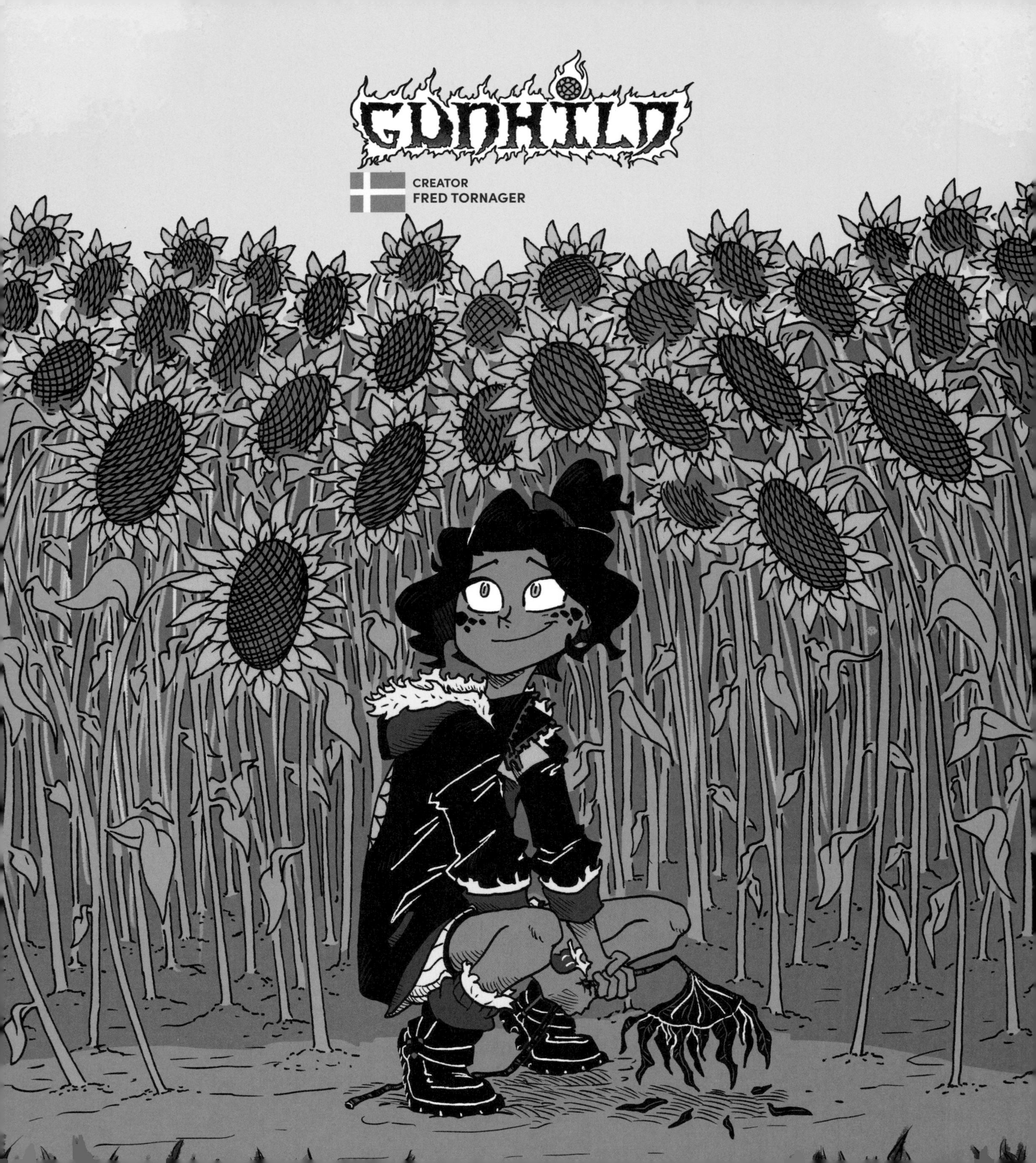
GUNHILD
CREATOR
FRED TORNAGER

GUNHILD

NAME: GUNHILD
OF THE SUNFLOWER

HEIGHT: 4'6"

SERIES: GUNHILD

BIO: Gunhild is muspel, a
tiny wildfire personified.
Desperate to earn others'
respect, Gunhild charges
ahead, stubborn and
steadfast in pursuing her
sense of justice.

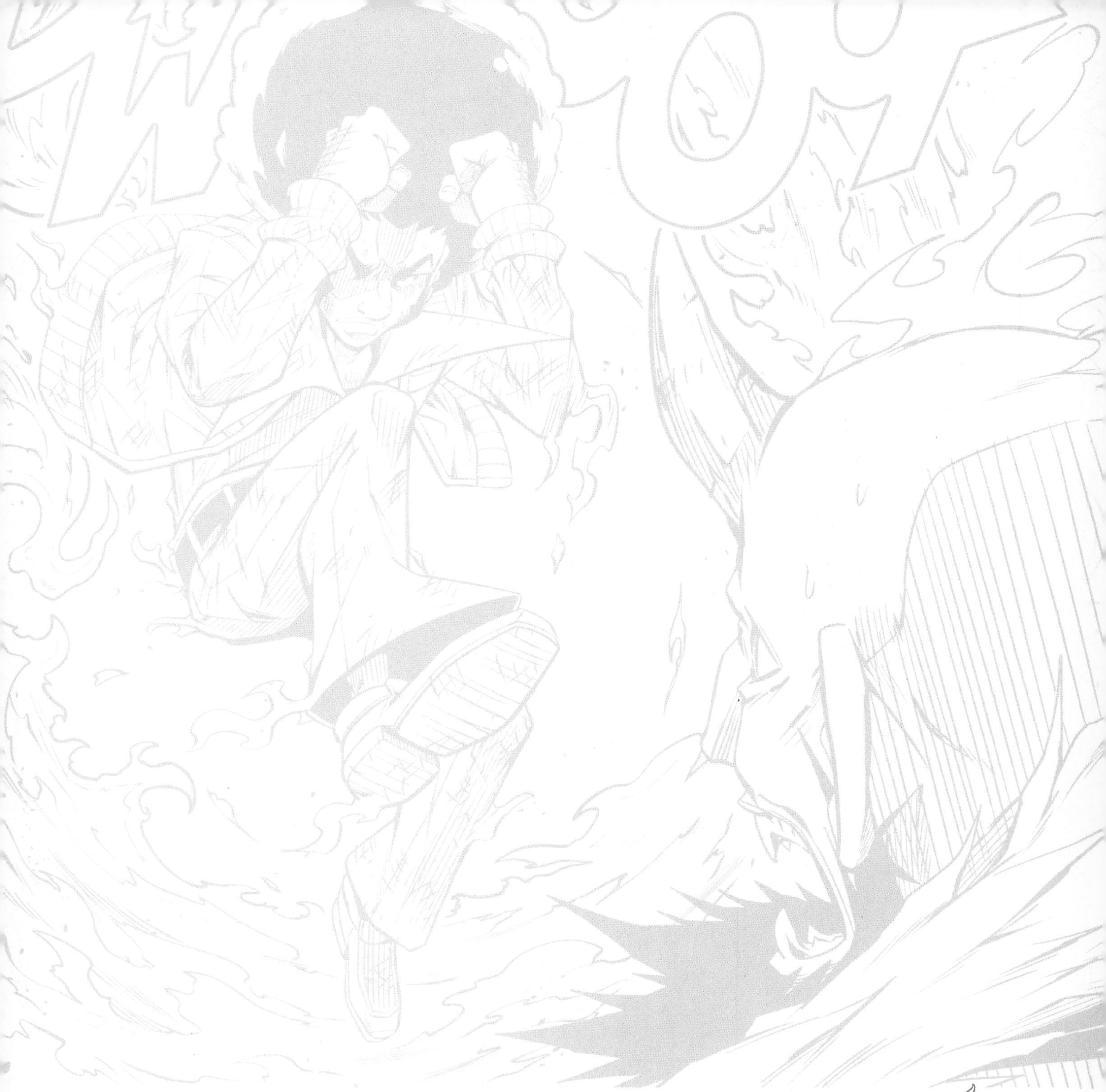

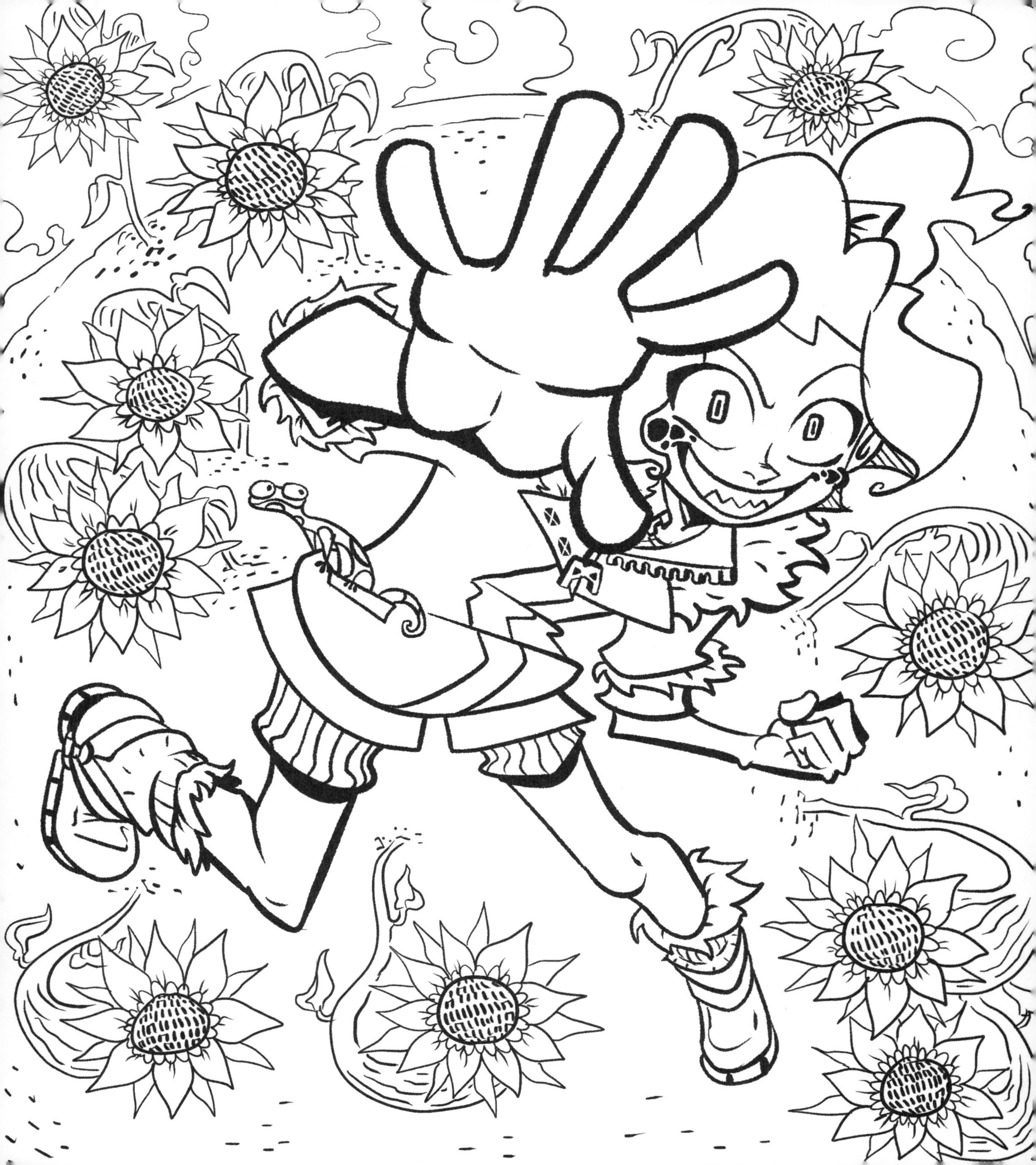

GUNHILD

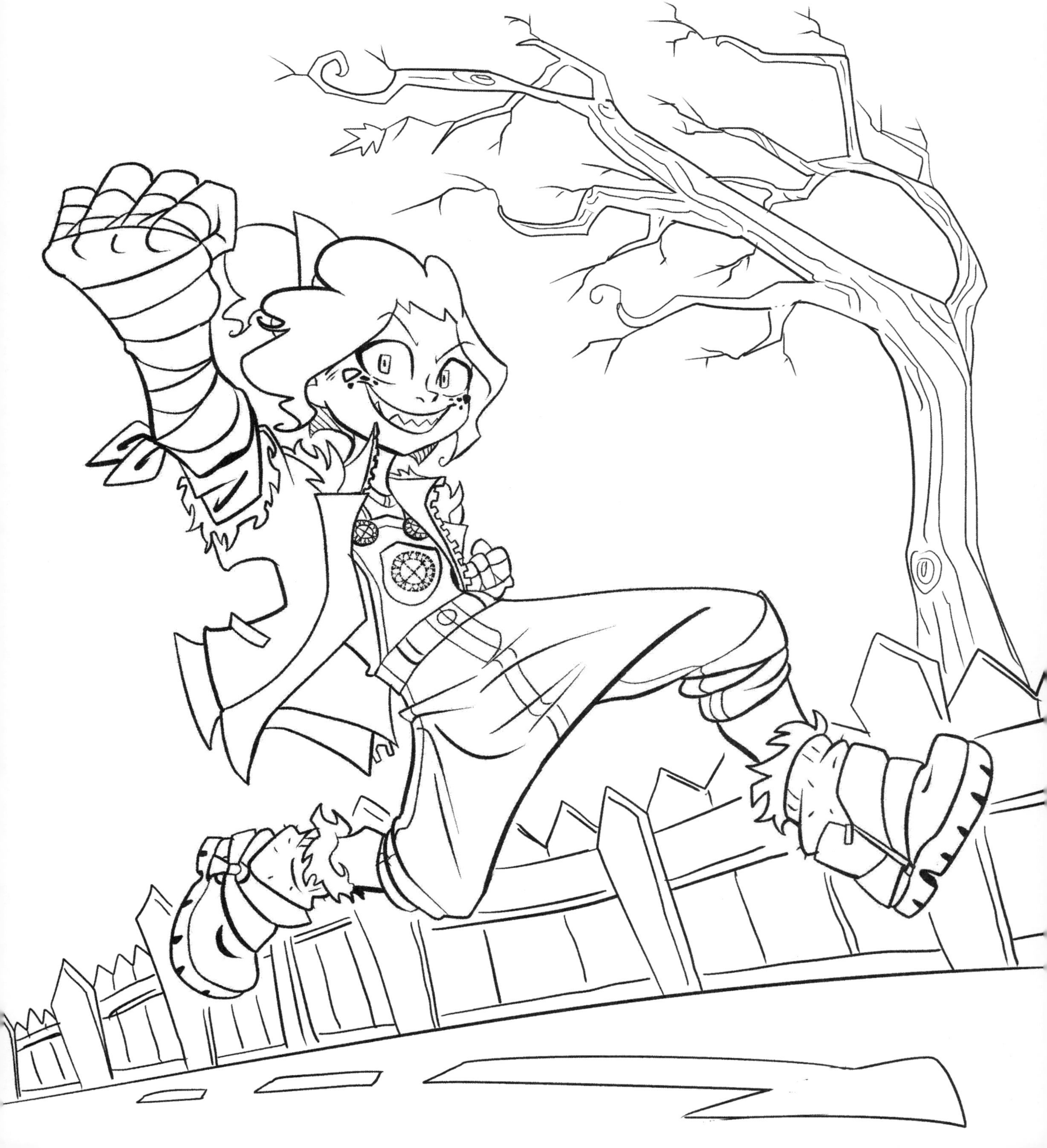

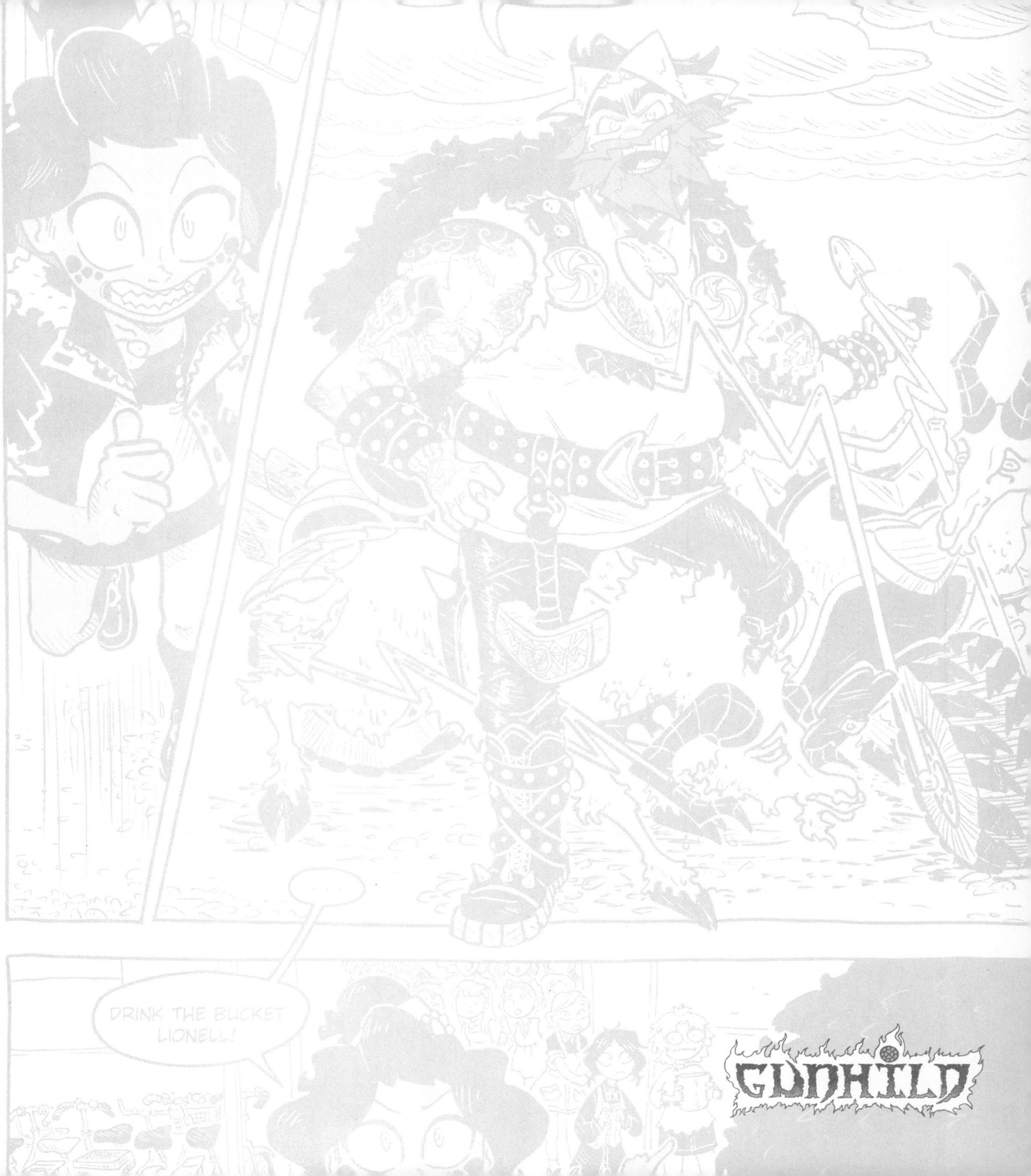
DRINK THE BUCKET
LIONELL!

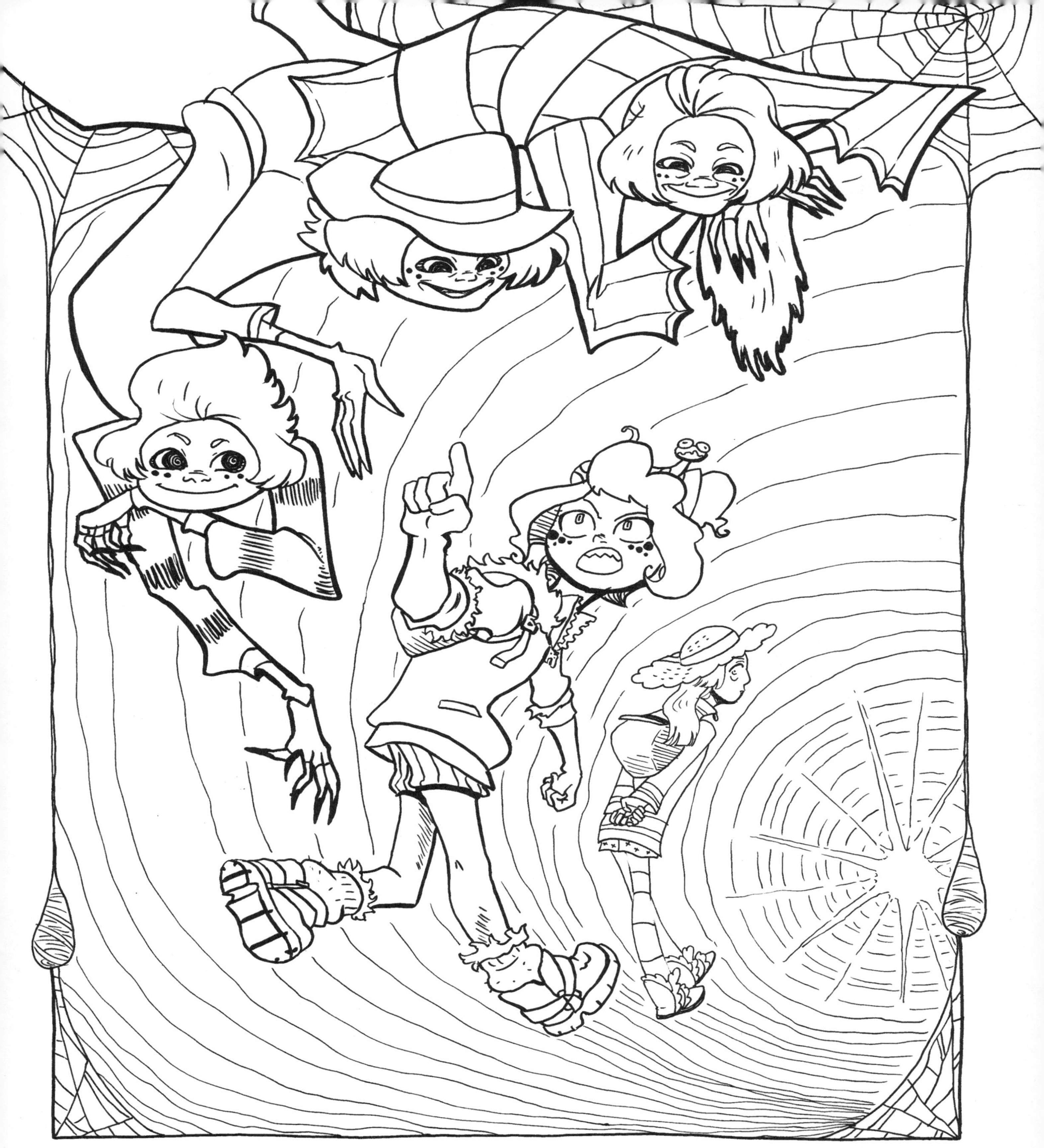

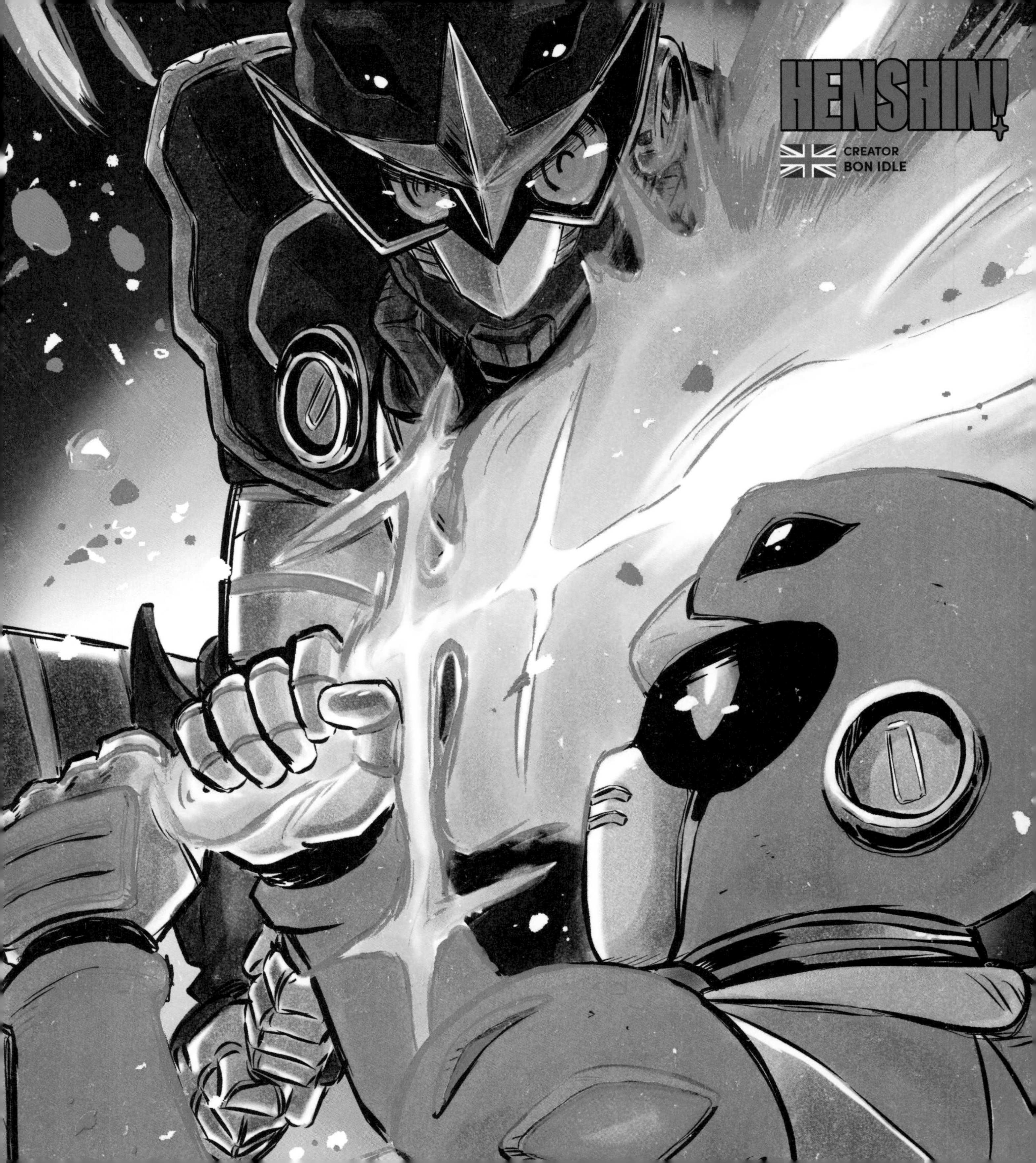
HENSHIN!
CREATOR
BON IDLE

BLAZE

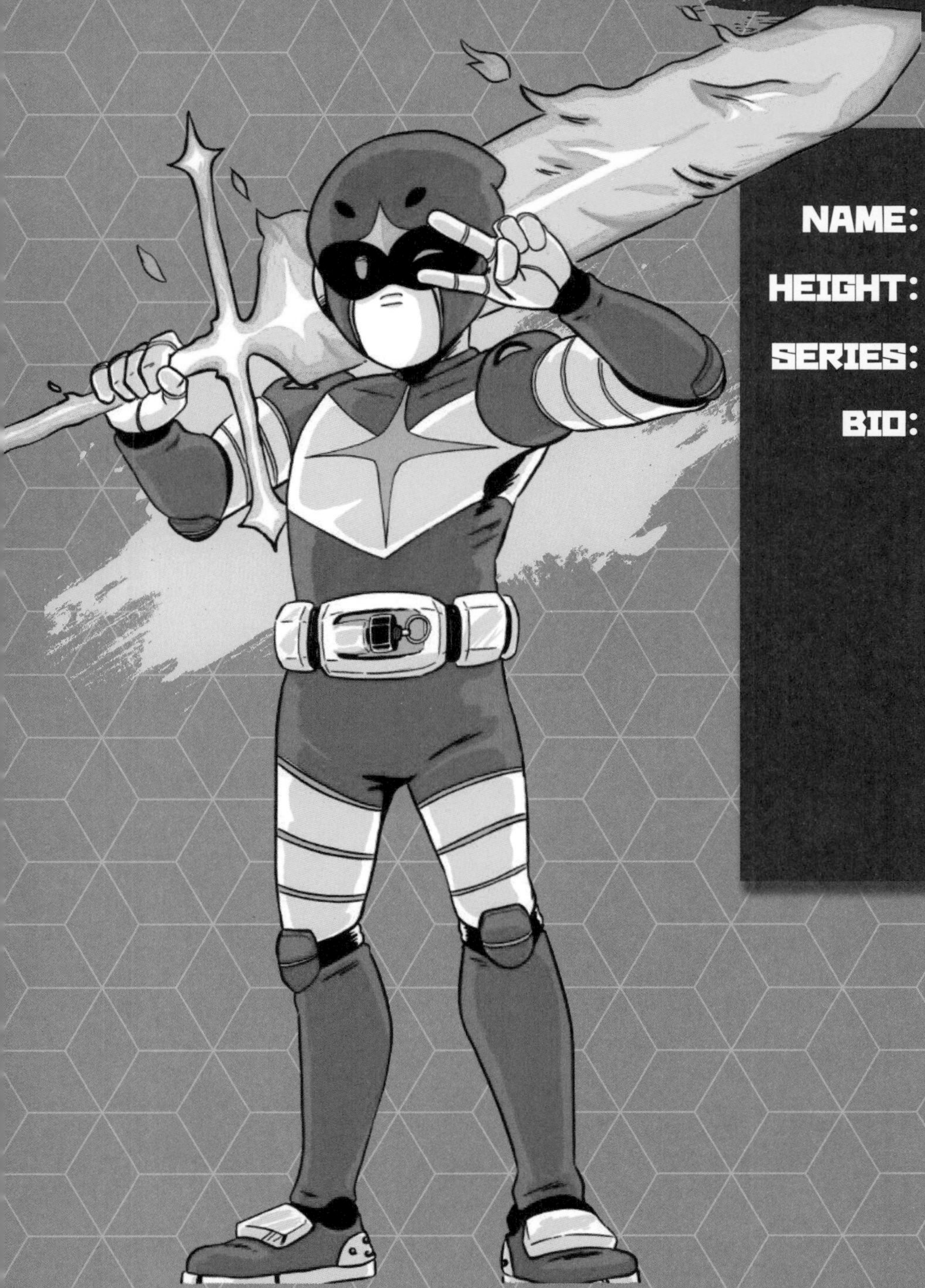

NAME: BLAZE (ALEX NOLAN)

HEIGHT: 5'10"

SERIES: HENSHIN!

BIO: Earnest and good-hearted if a little scatterbrained, Alex is navigating life as a gay man as he studies to become a journalist. When a Kaiju attacks his city and he encounters the Masked Hero, the hero transfers his power, enabling Alex to become a Reikaiger by saying the word "Henshin!," thus transforming into the phoenix hero BLAZE.

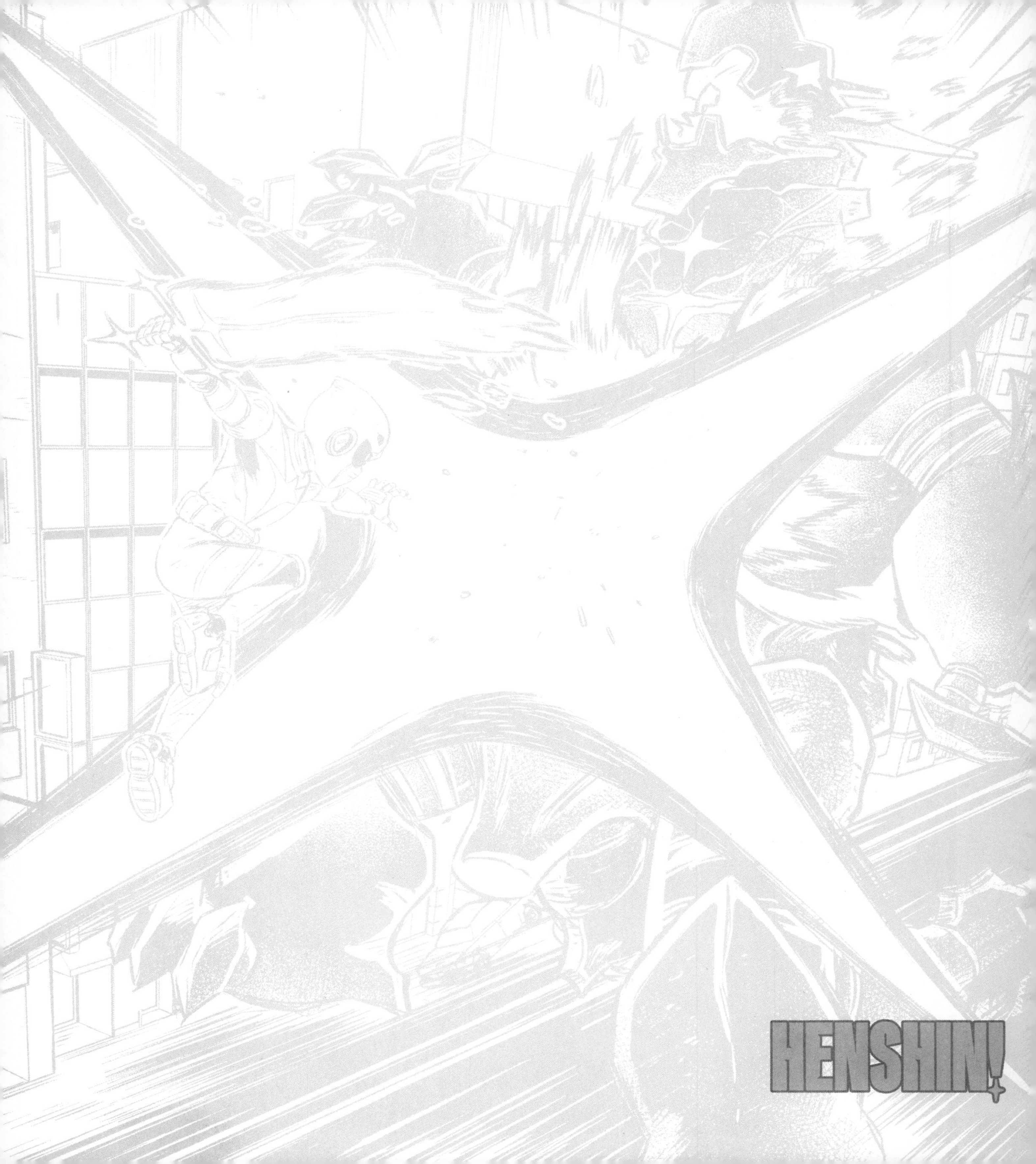
HENSHIN!

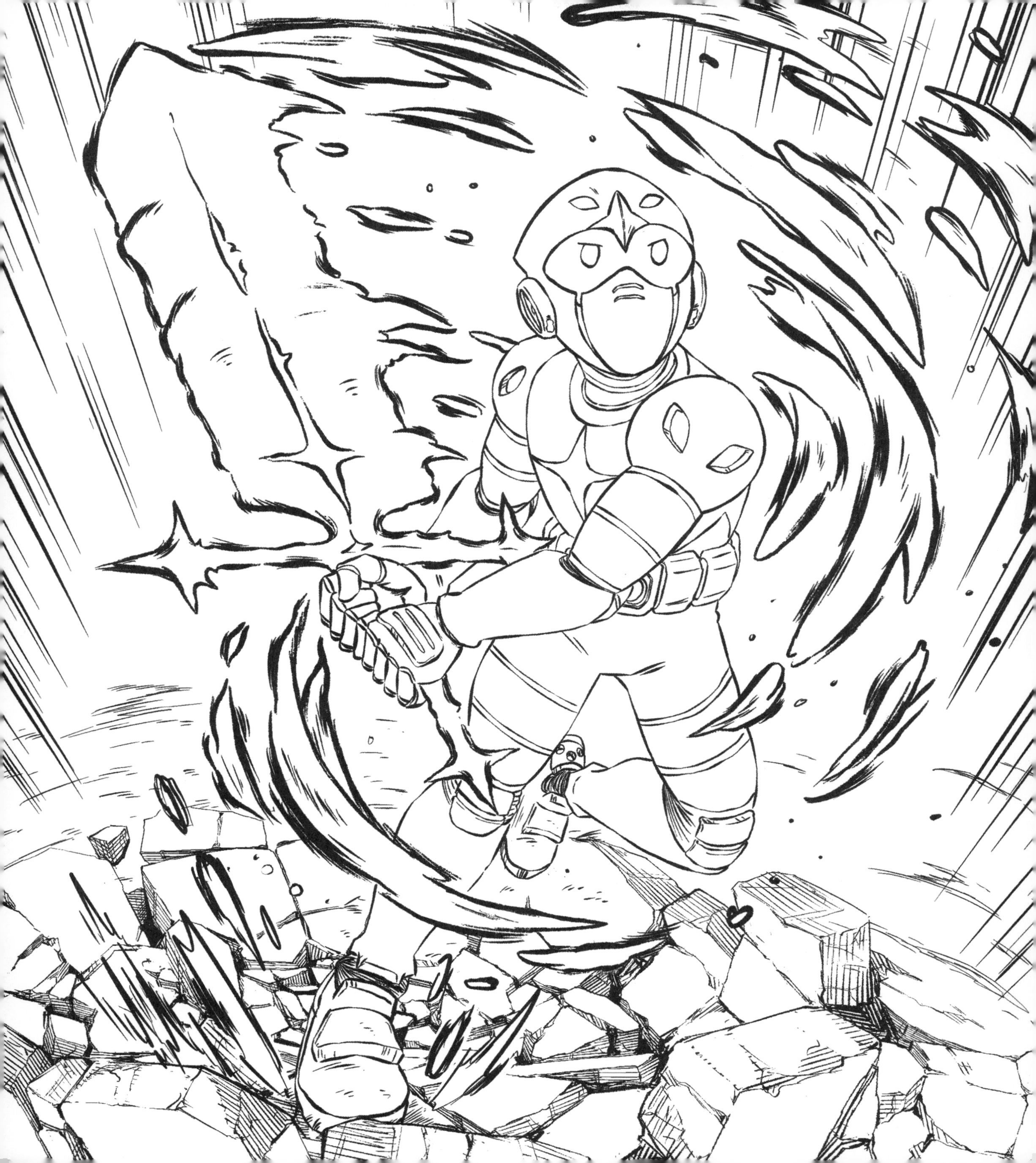

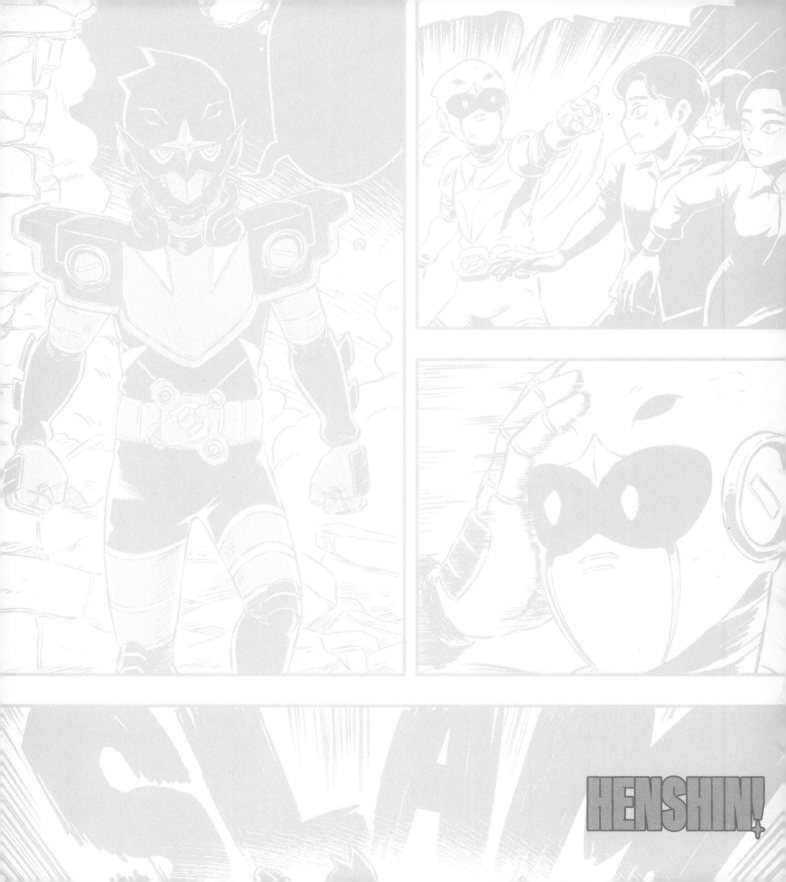

HENSHIN!

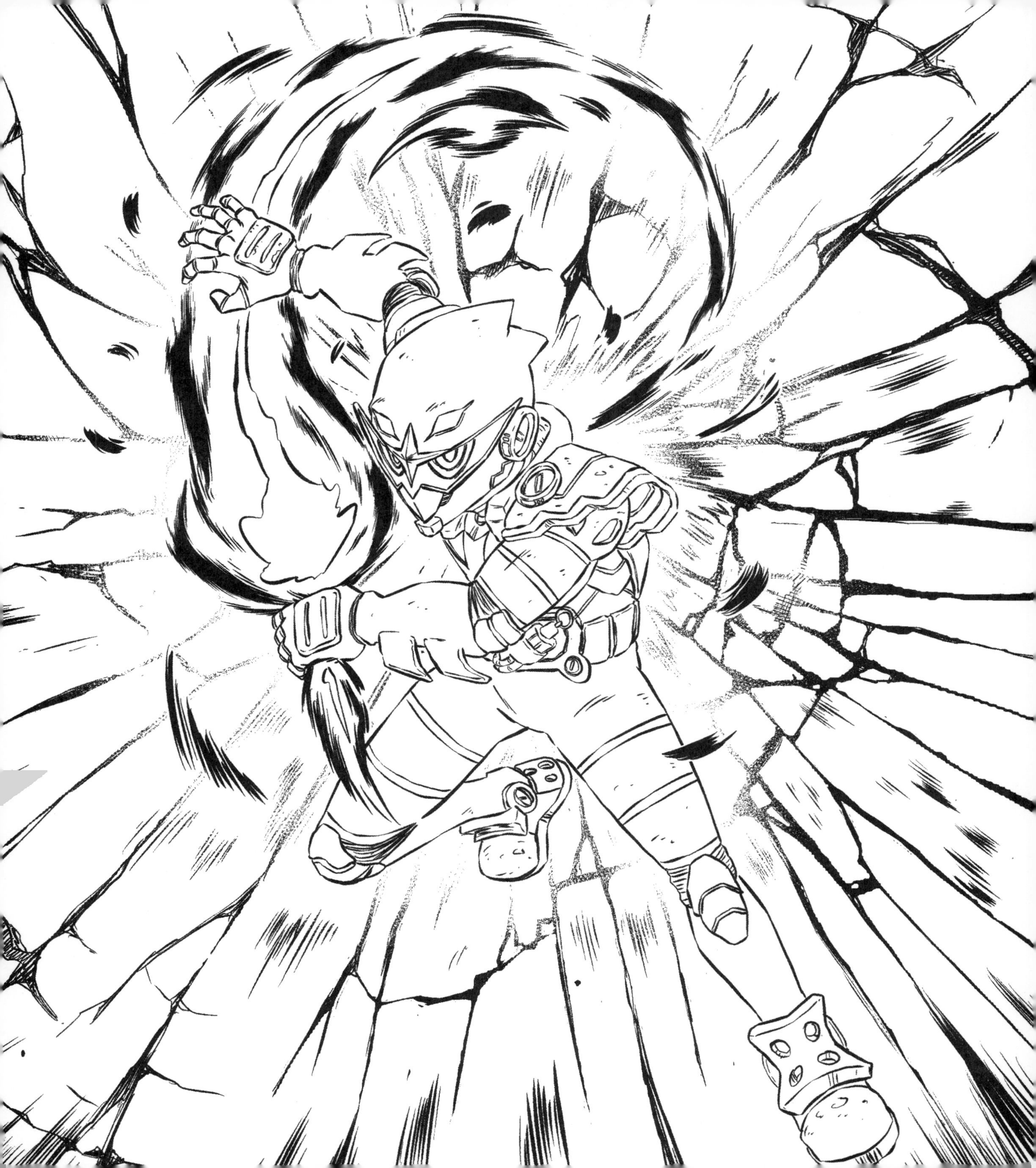

ORISHA

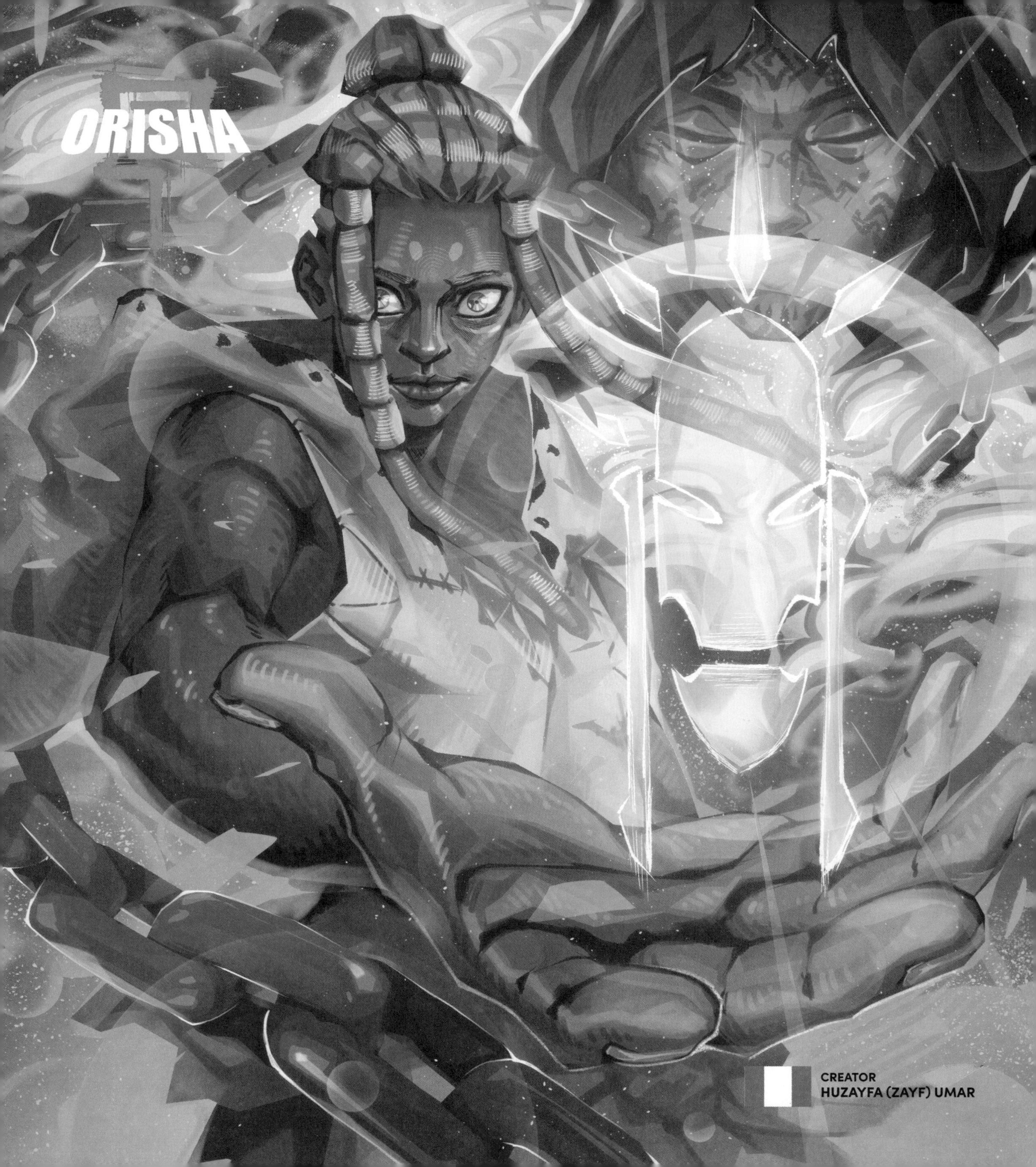

CREATOR
HUZAYFA (ZAYF) UMAR

ABOKI

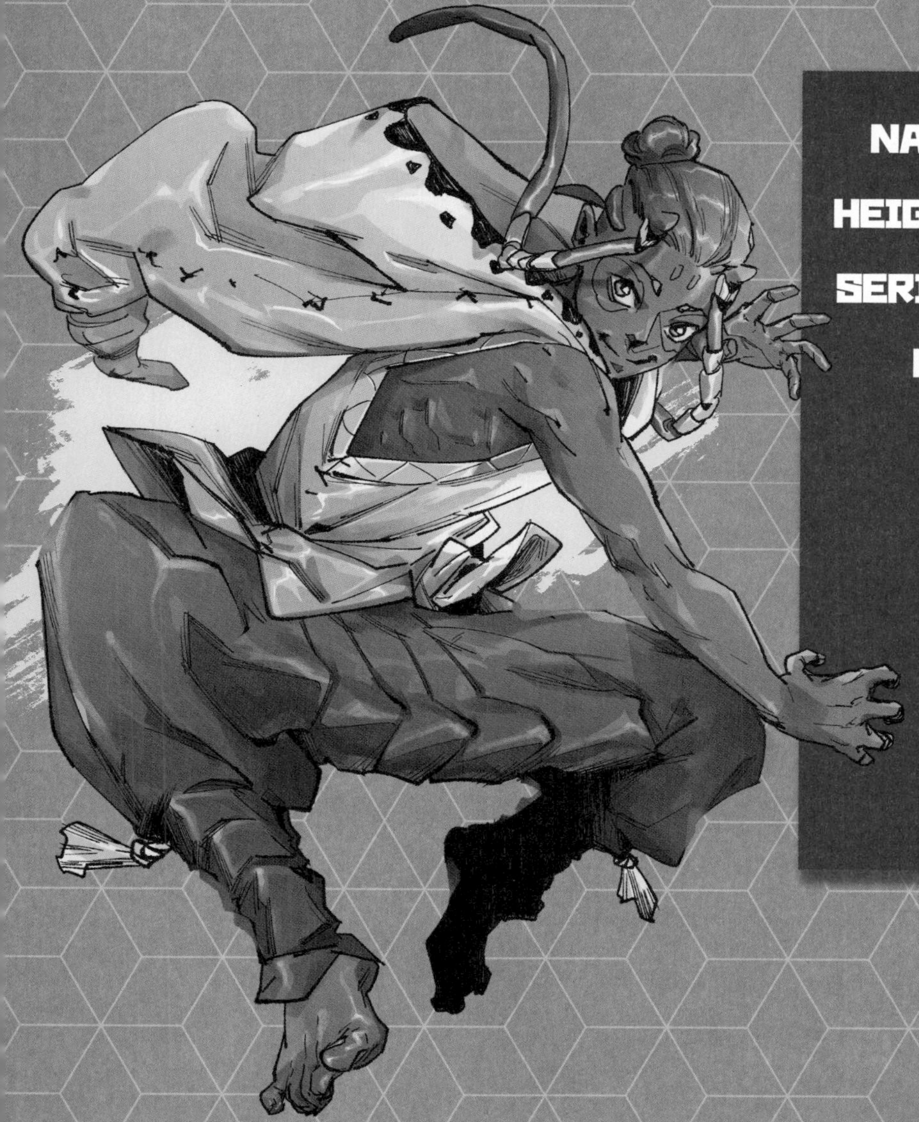

NAME: ABOKI

HEIGHT: 5’8”

SERIES: ORISHA

BIO: Chosen to become one of five prime Orisha, Aboki is compassionate and seeks out peace over violence--but has a darker side when pushed over the edge. He’s had no exposure to the outside world, making him very naive, and while he isn’t a genius, he uses his power of the cosmic seed to manipulate matter in a smart and crafty way.

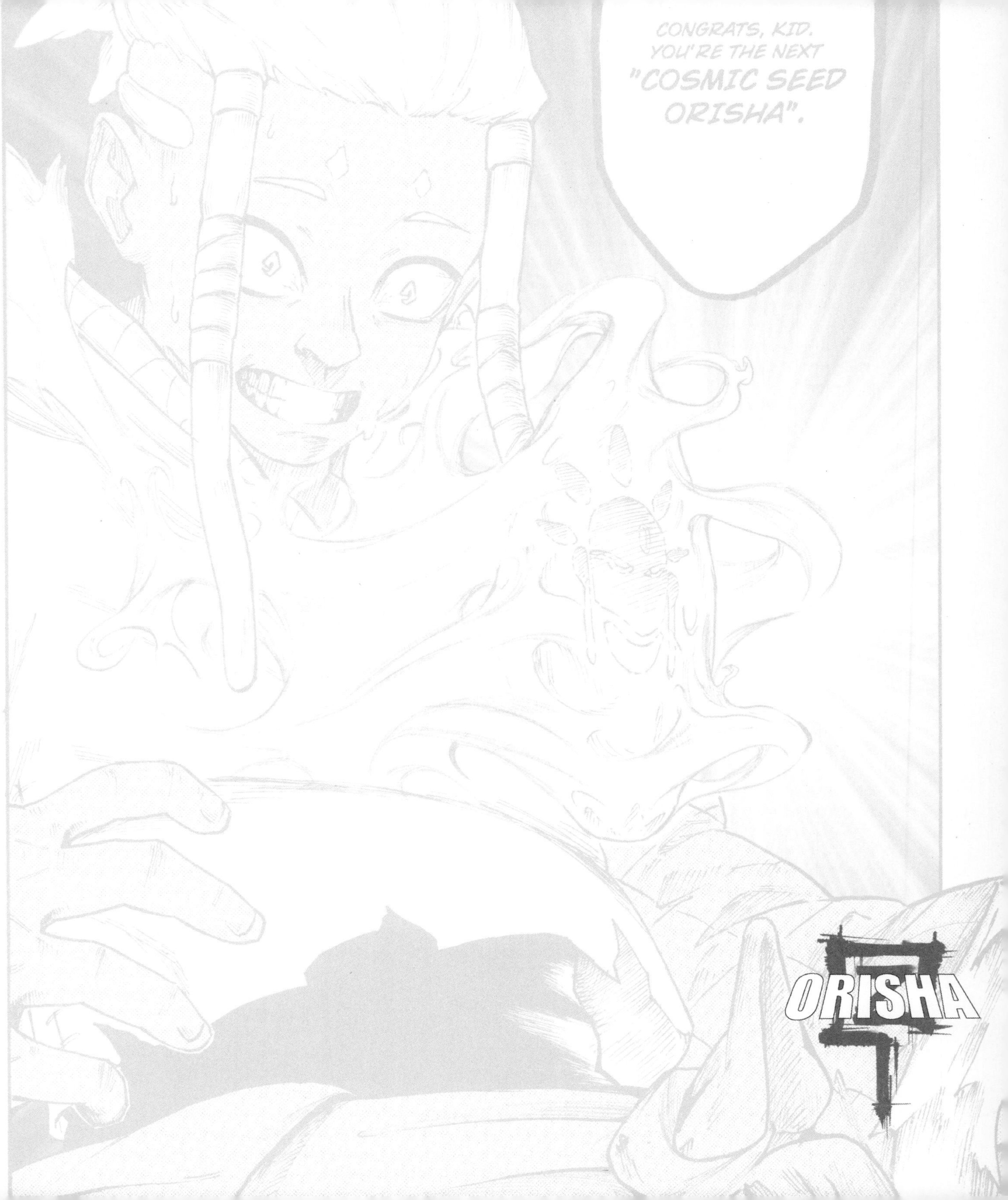
CONGRATS, KID. YOU'RE THE NEXT "COSMIC SEED ORISHA".
ORISHA

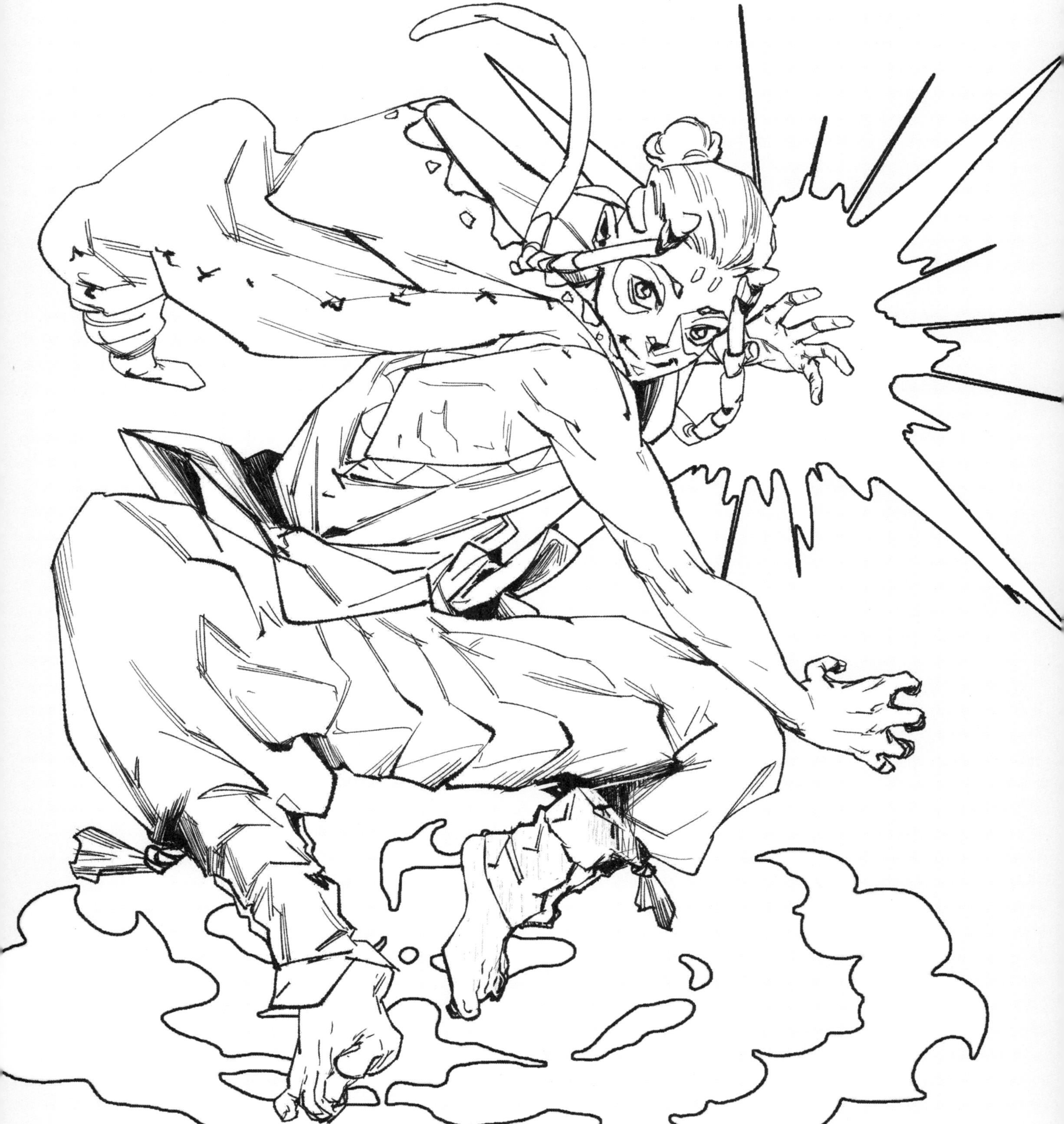

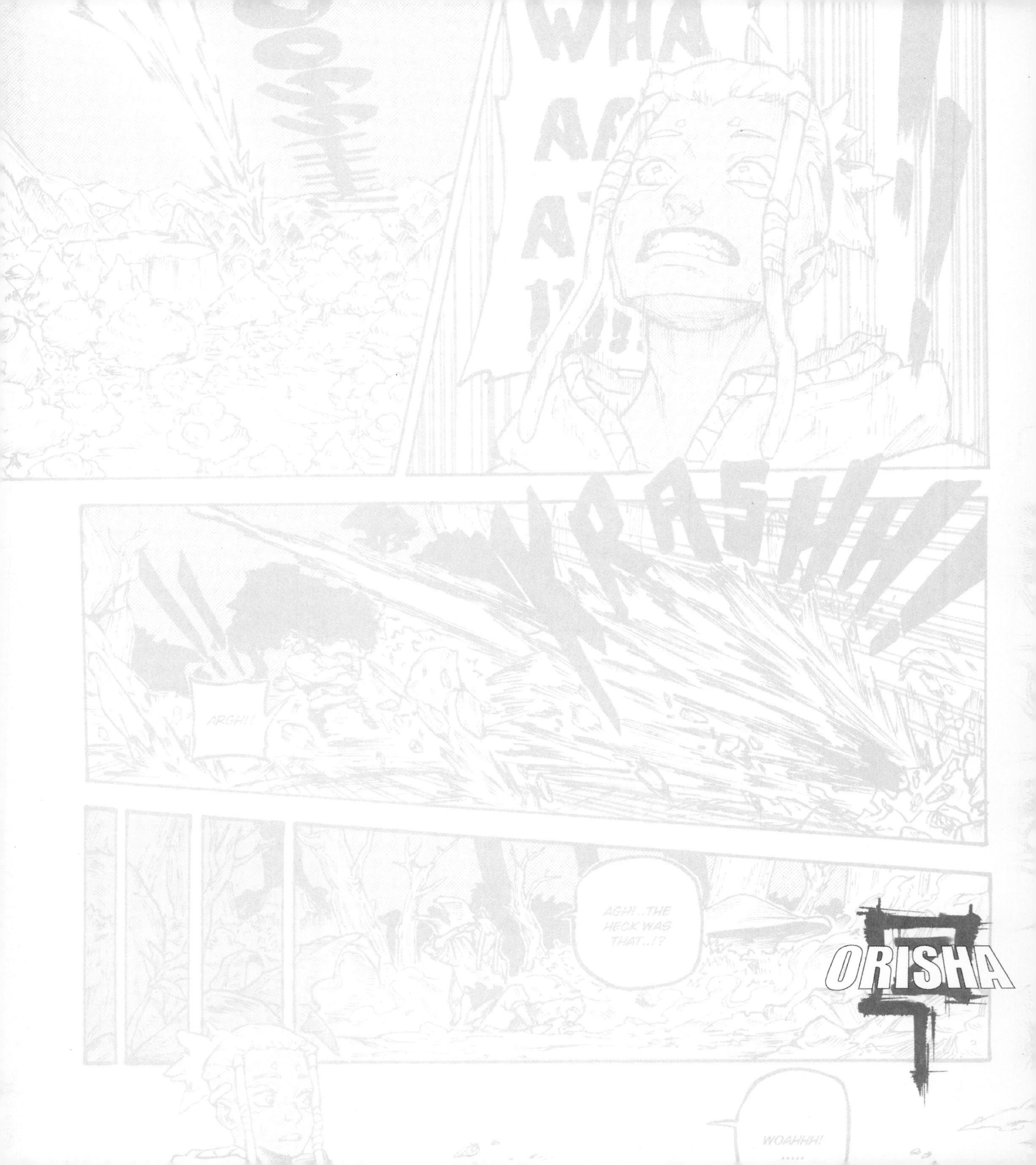
WHA
ARGH!!
AGH!..THE HECK WAS THAT..!?
ORISHA
WOAHHH!
.....

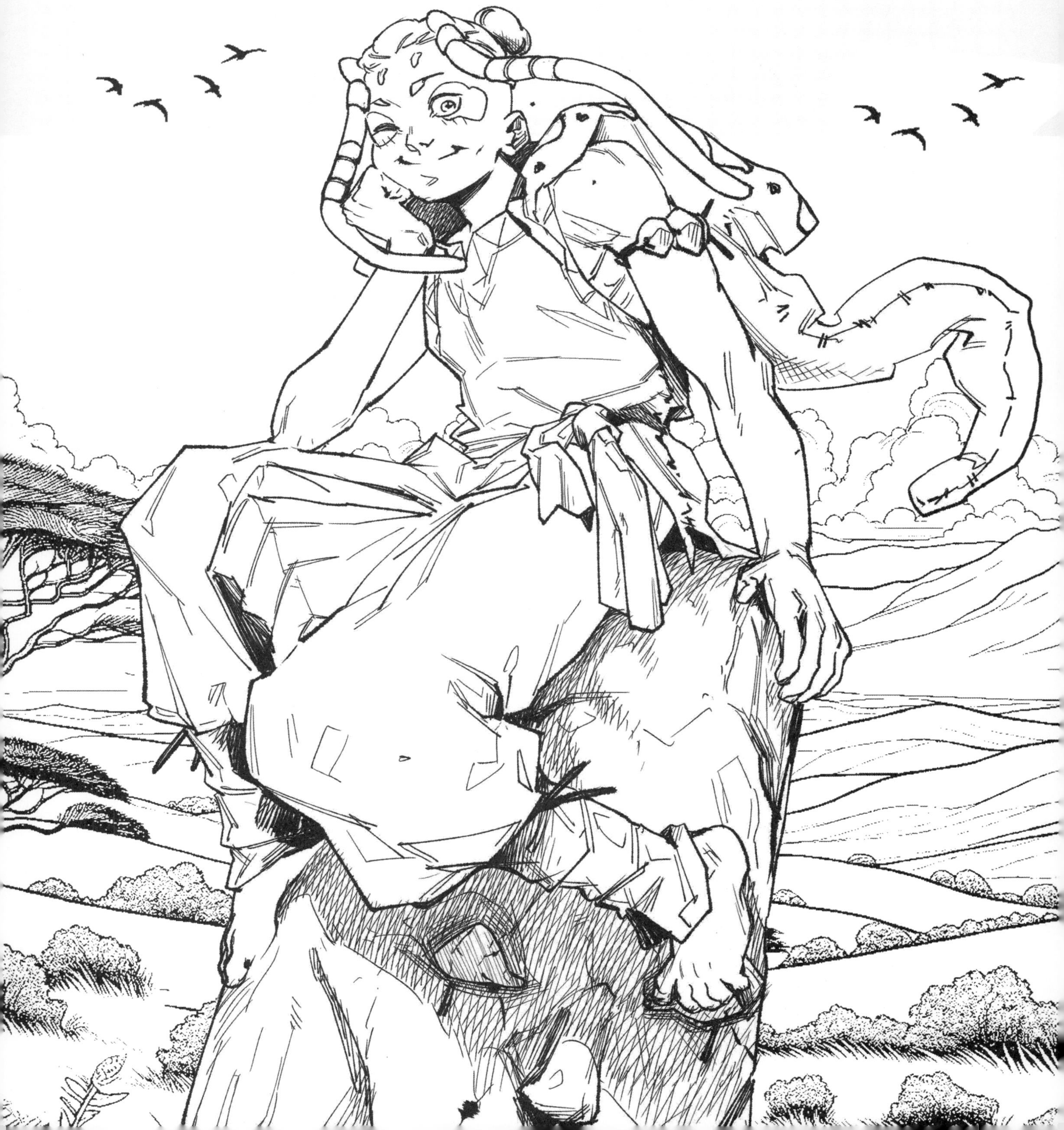

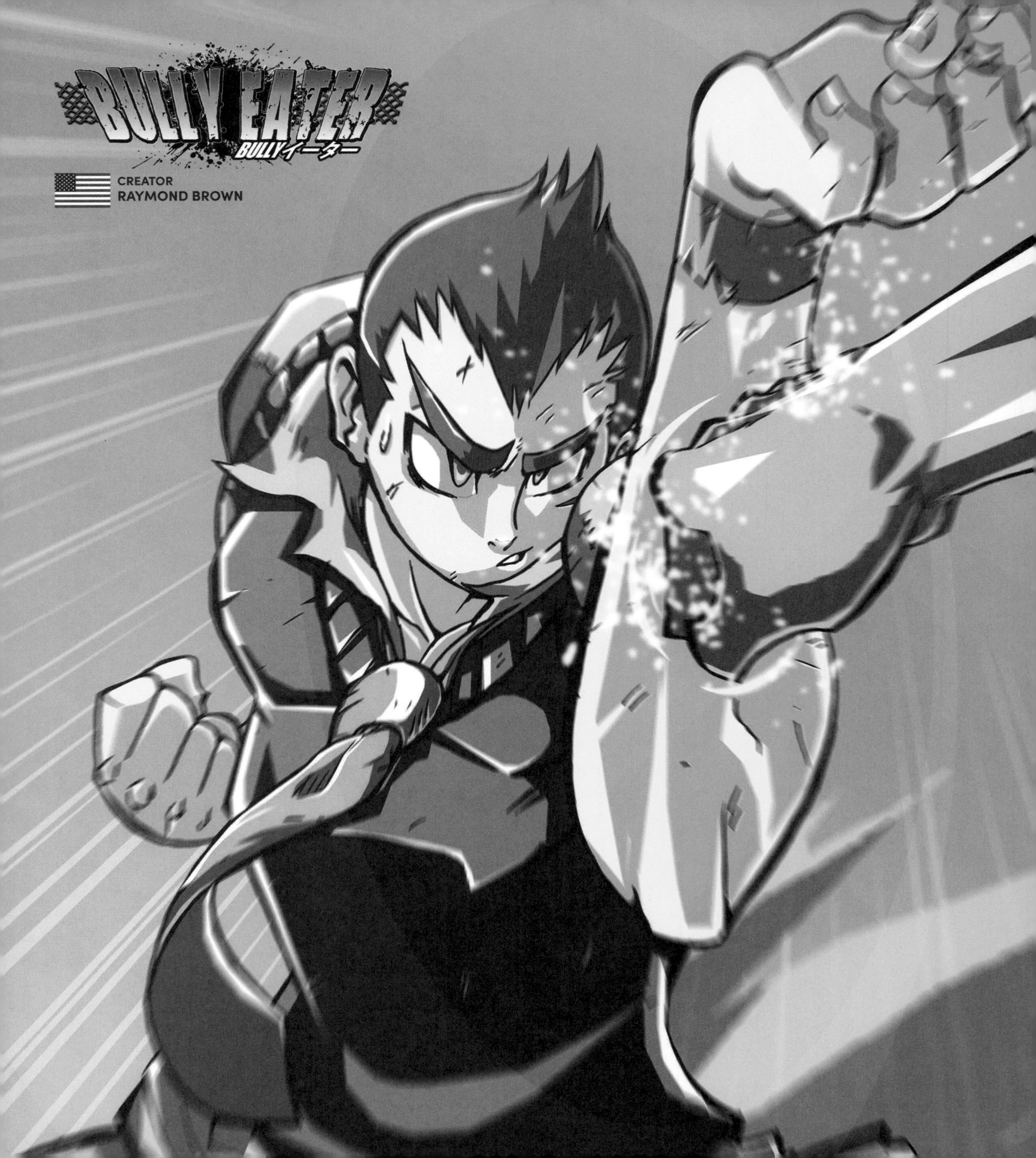
BULLY EATER
BULLYイーター
CREATOR
RAYMOND BROWN

ISAO

NAME: ISAO AKIA

HEIGHT: 6'1"

SERIES: BULLY EATER

BIO: Isao, a determined and spirited young martial artist, is deeply committed to safeguarding the weak. He is a student at the esteemed Greater Dragon Institute (GDI), renowned for its martial arts training. Although Isao isn't the top contender in terms of strength or speed, his resolve is unshaken in his pursuit to become the best in his class.

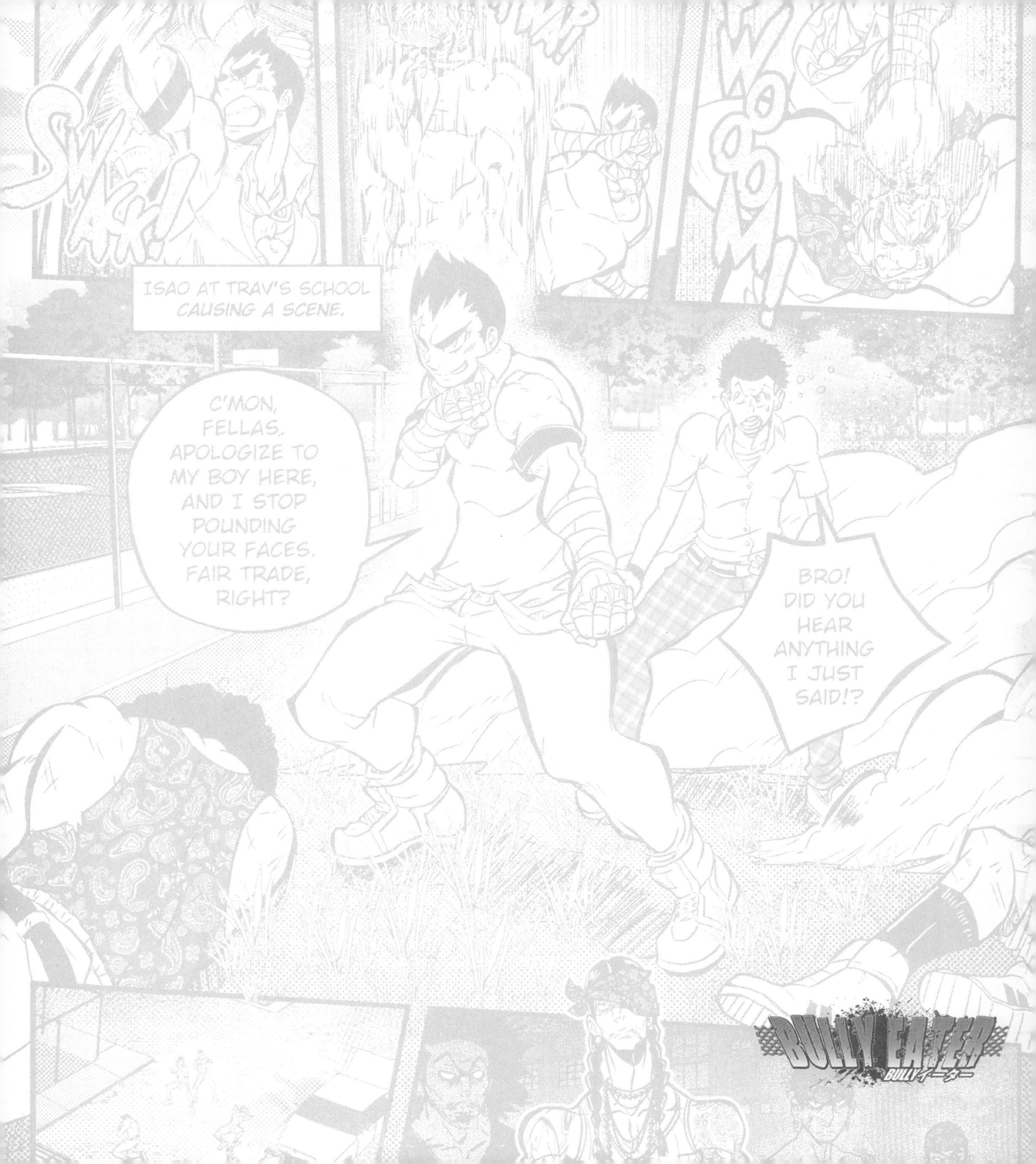
ISAO AT TRAV'S SCHOOL CAUSING A SCENE.
C'MON, FELLAS. APOLOGIZE TO MY BOY HERE, AND I STOP POUNDING YOUR FACES. FAIR TRADE, RIGHT?
BRO! DID YOU HEAR ANYTHING I JUST SAID!?
BULLY EATER

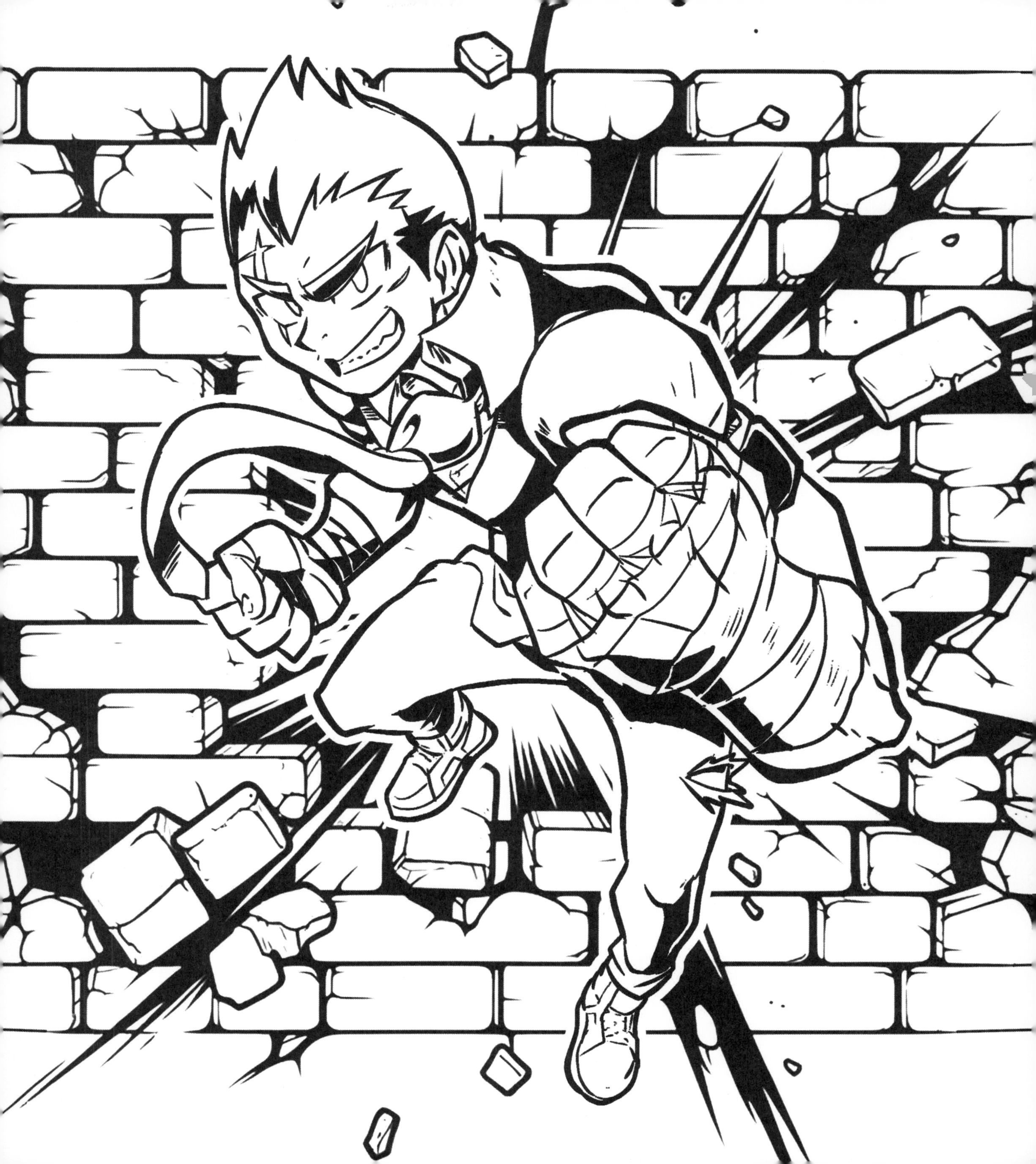

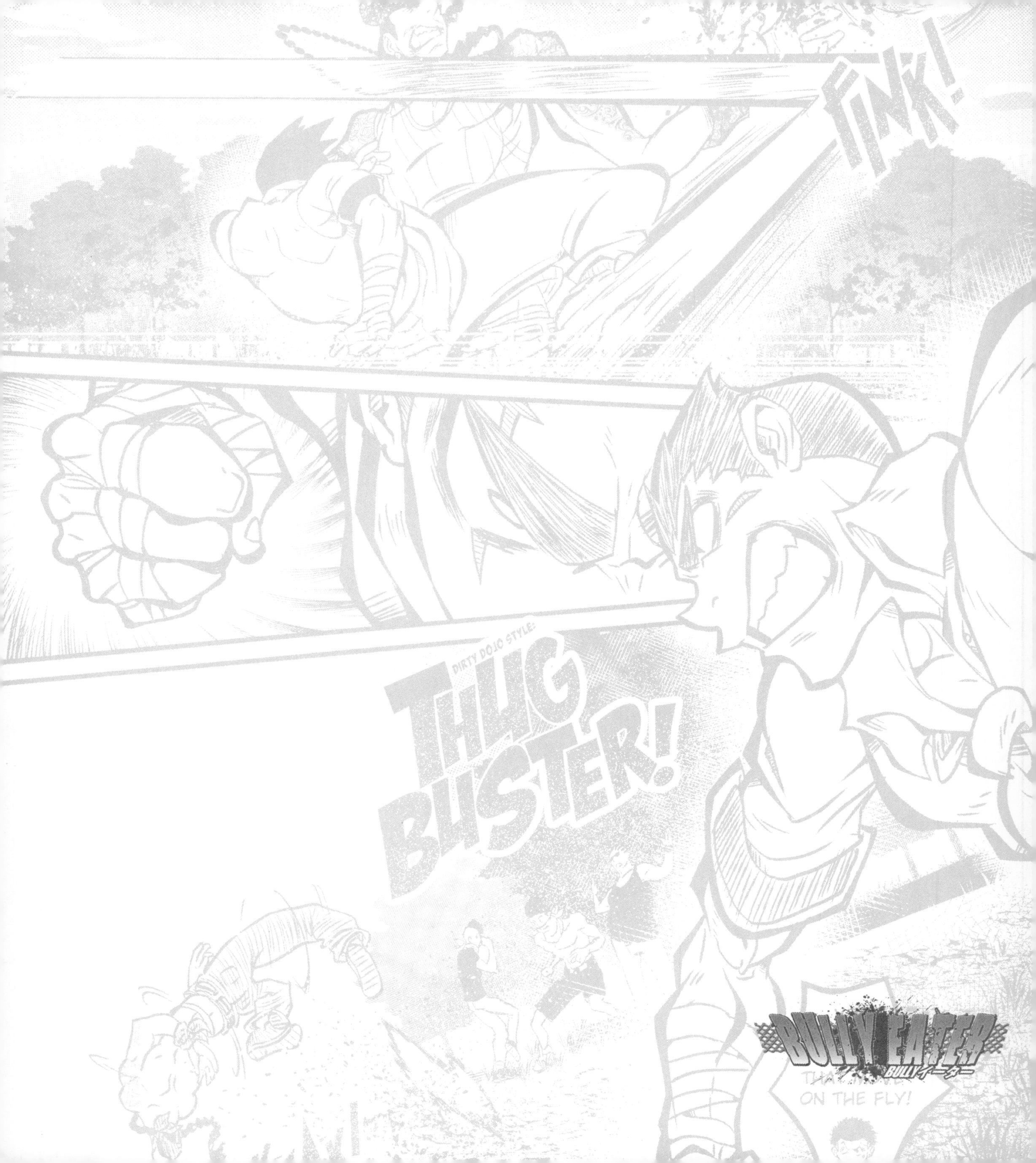
FINK!
DIRTY DOJO STYLE:
THUG BUSTER!
BULLY EATER
BULLYイーター
ON THE FLY!

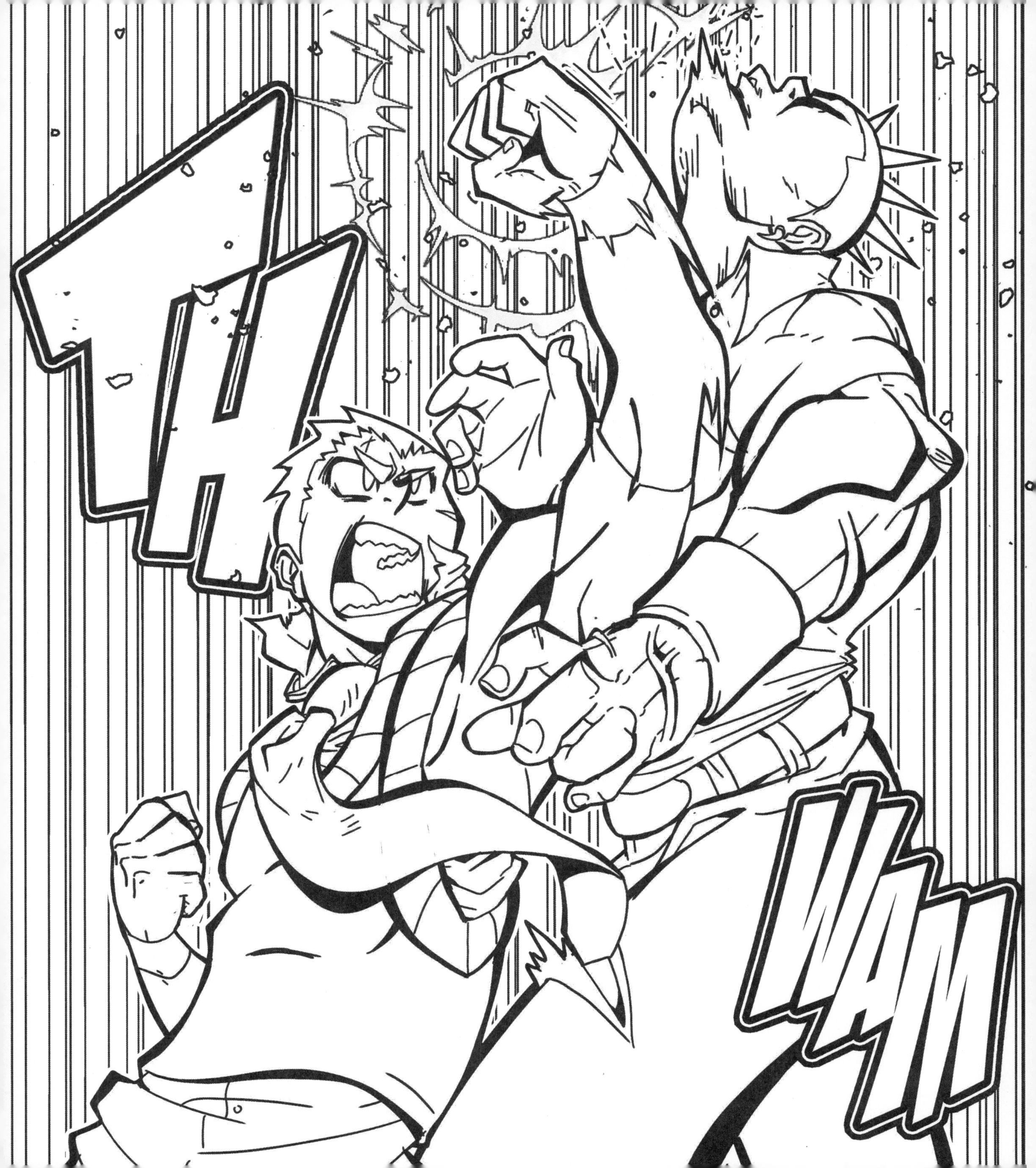
TH
WAM

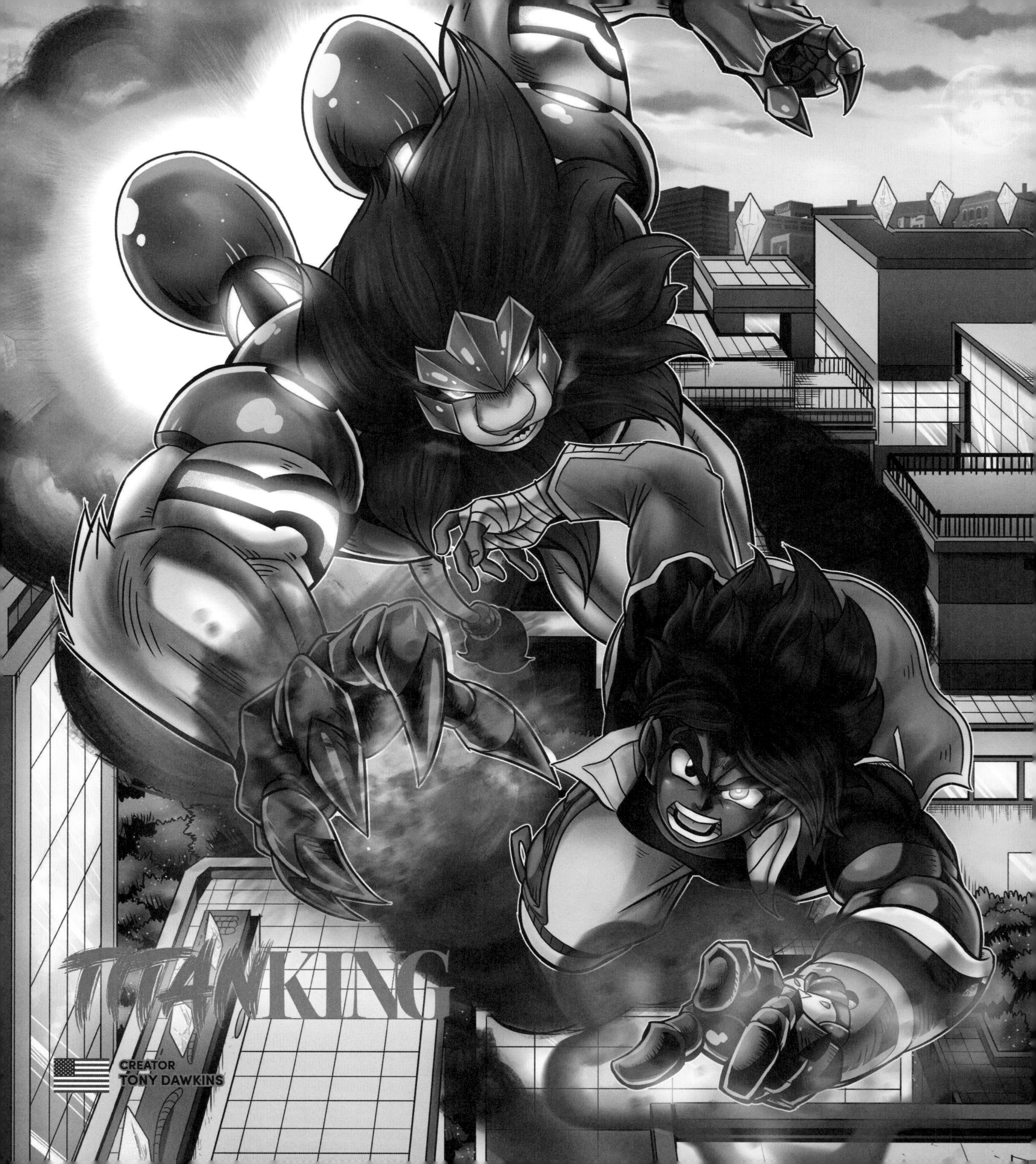
TITANKING
CREATOR
TONY DAWKINS

ELI & REXLEO

NAME: ELI SANTOS & REXLEO

HEIGHT: 5'9" (Eli)

SERIES: TITAN KING

BIO: Eli, a teenager with a fiery temperament and a heart of gold, is a natural fighter. He skillfully uses his special ability to generate vibrations to confront his enemies. When facing overwhelming challenges, he can call upon his powerful Titan ally, Rexleo, to join him in battle.

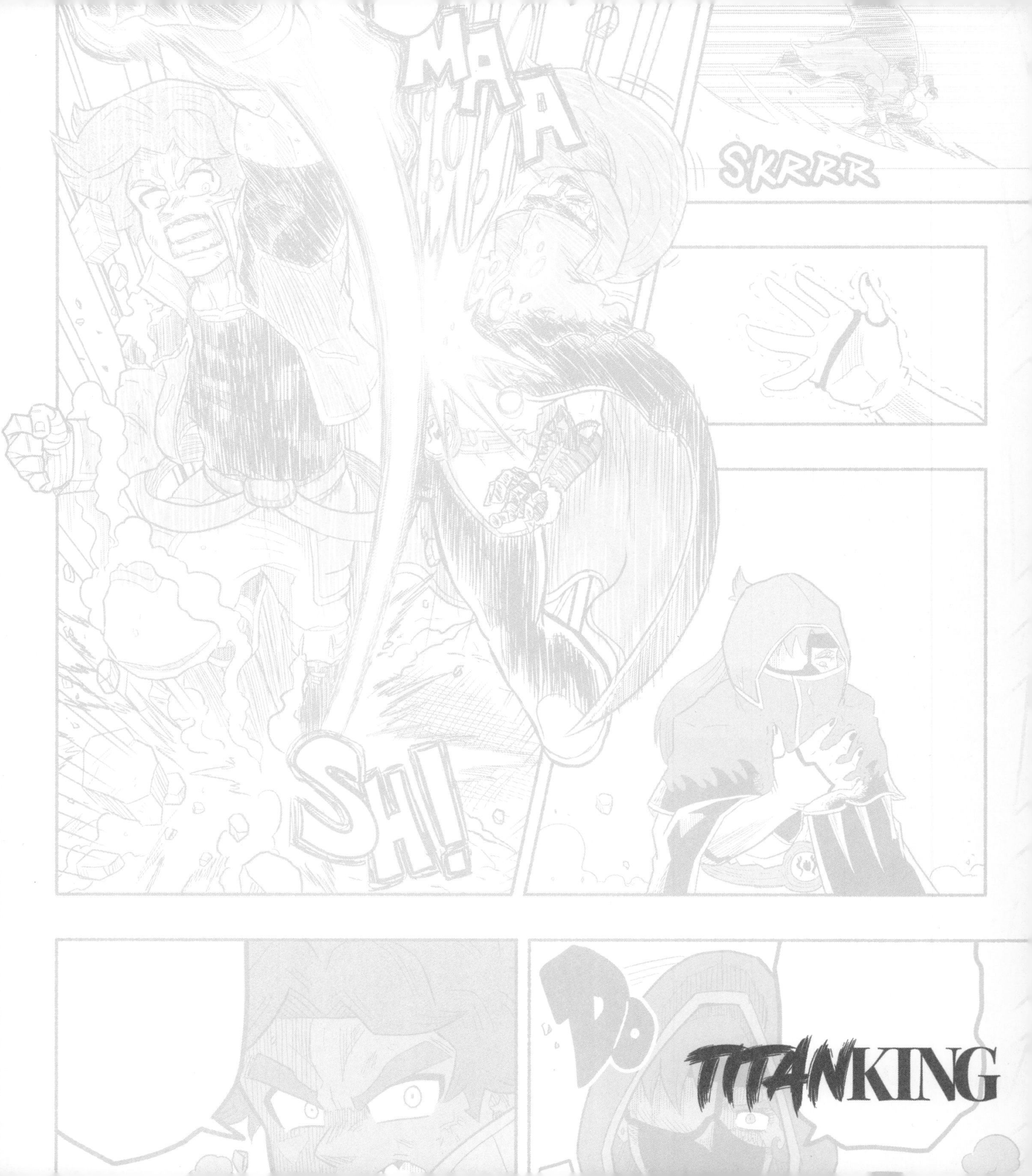
MAA
SKRRR
SH!
DO
TITANKING

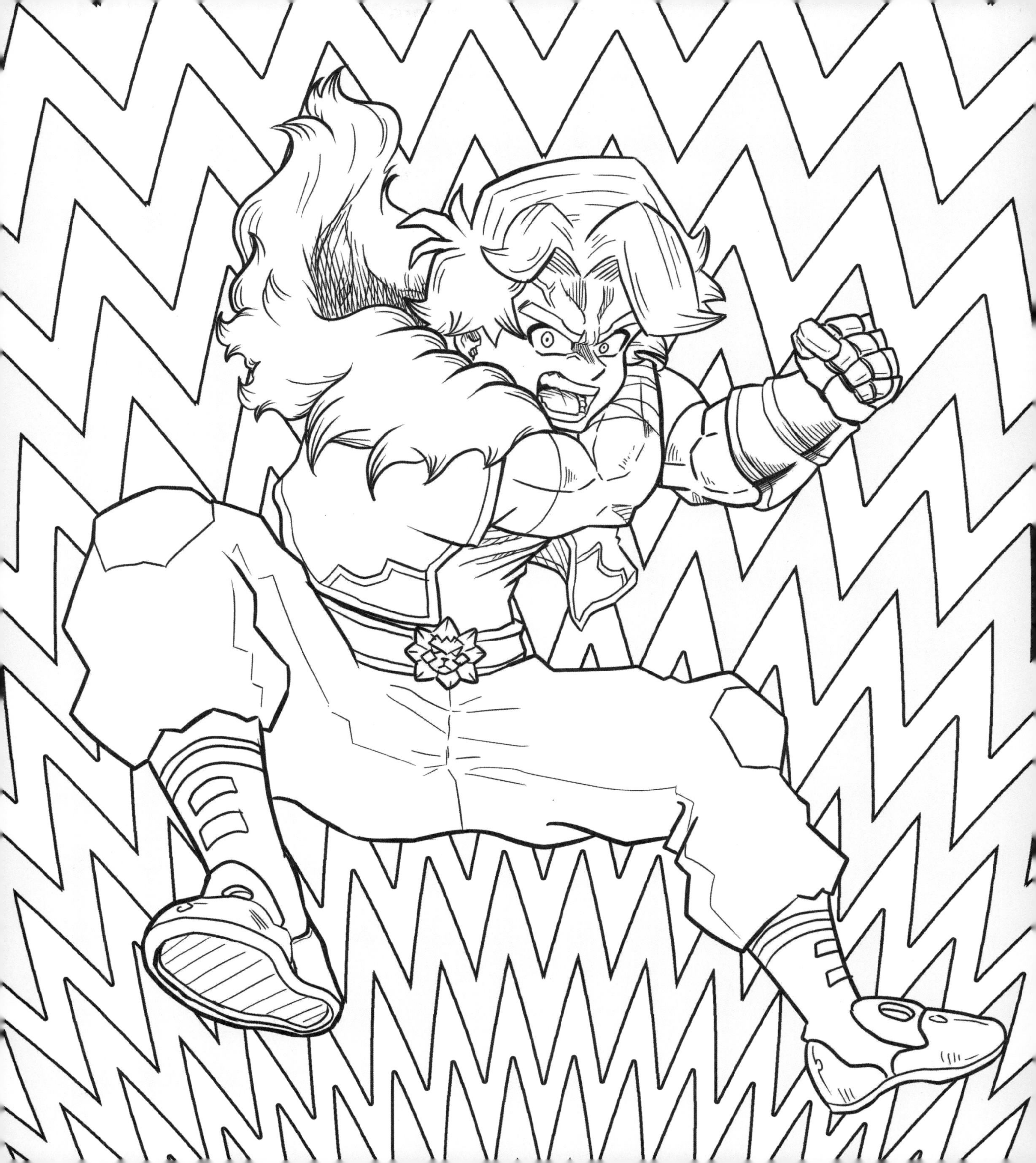

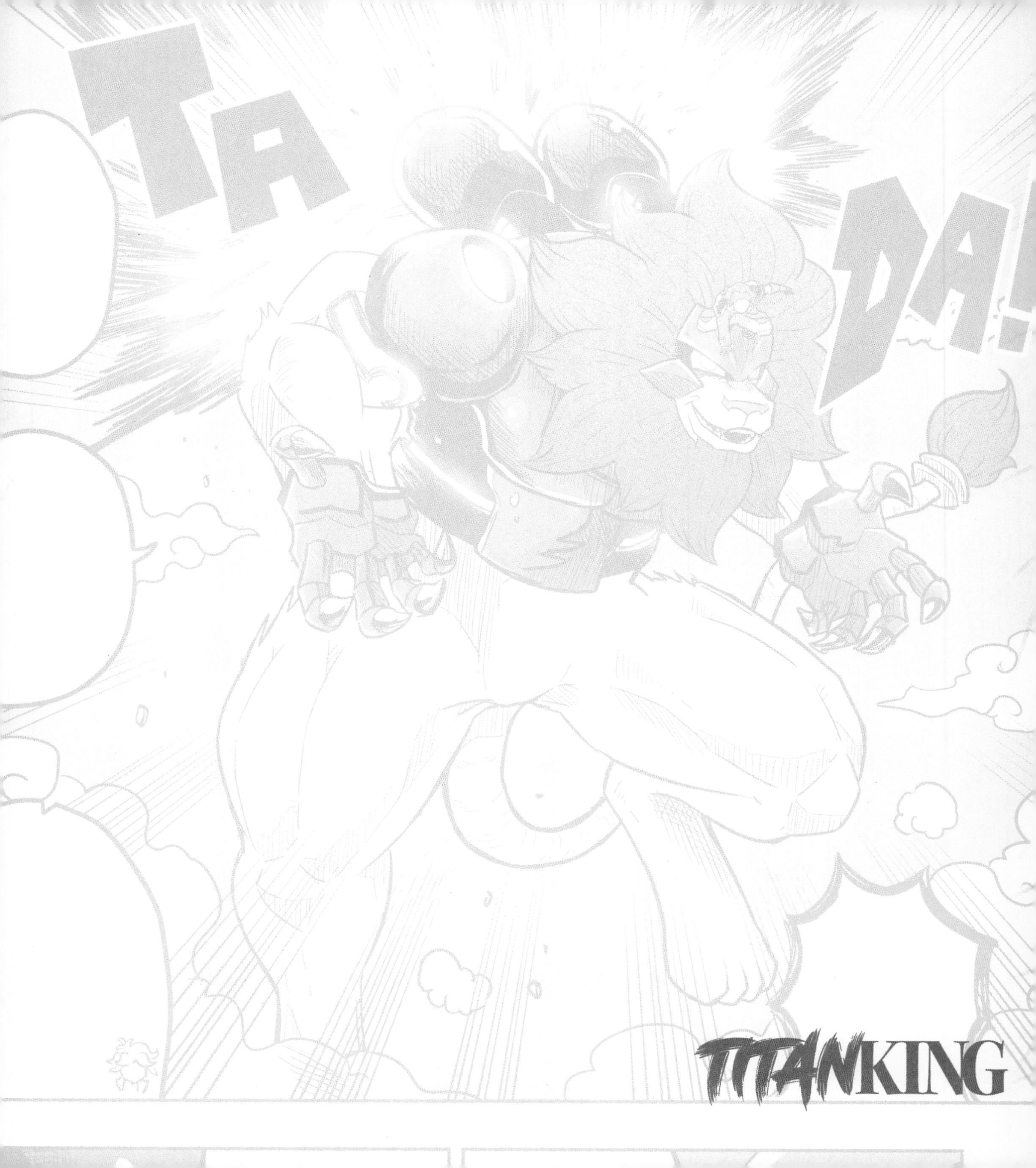
TA
DA!

TITANKING

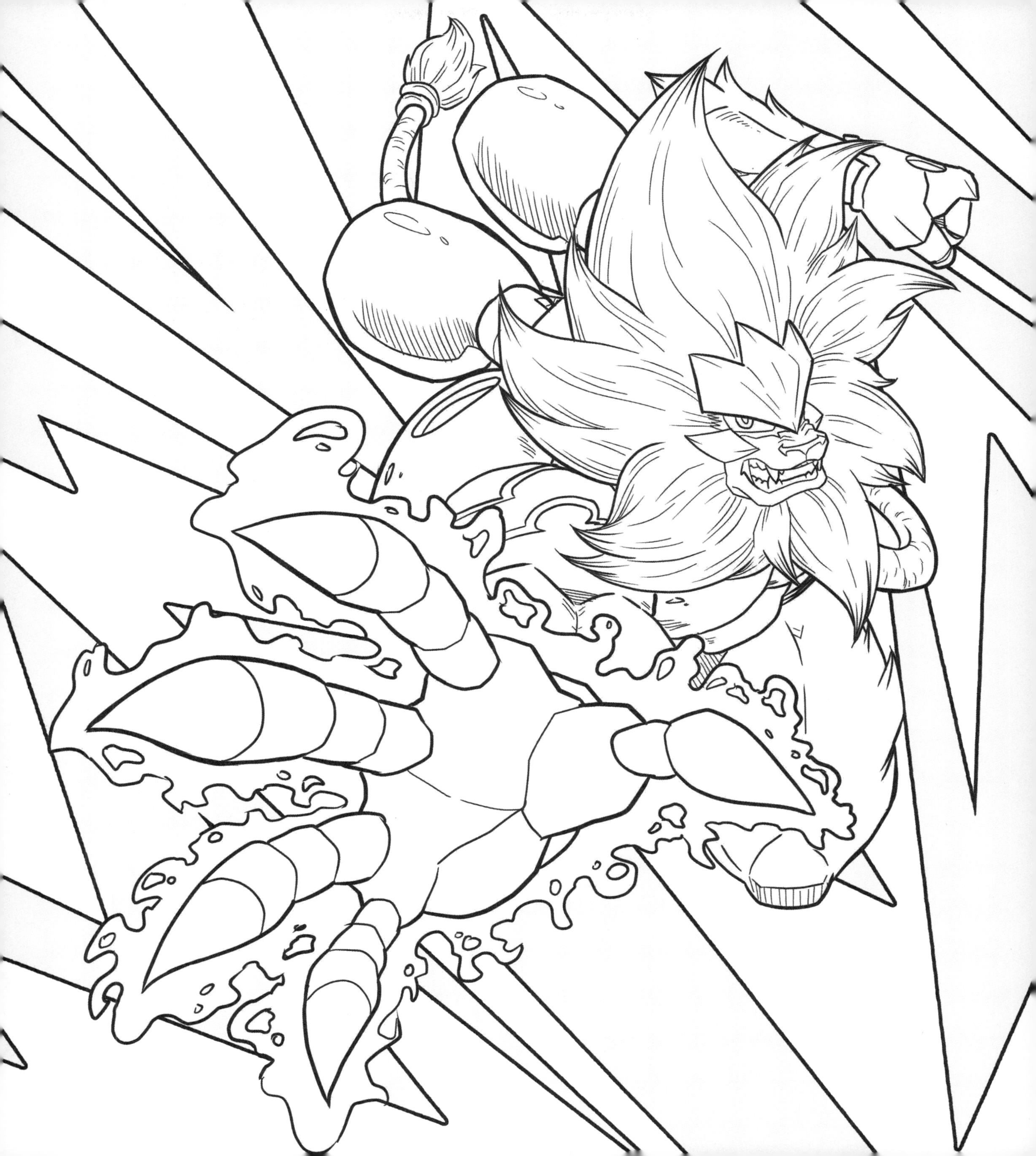

WARS

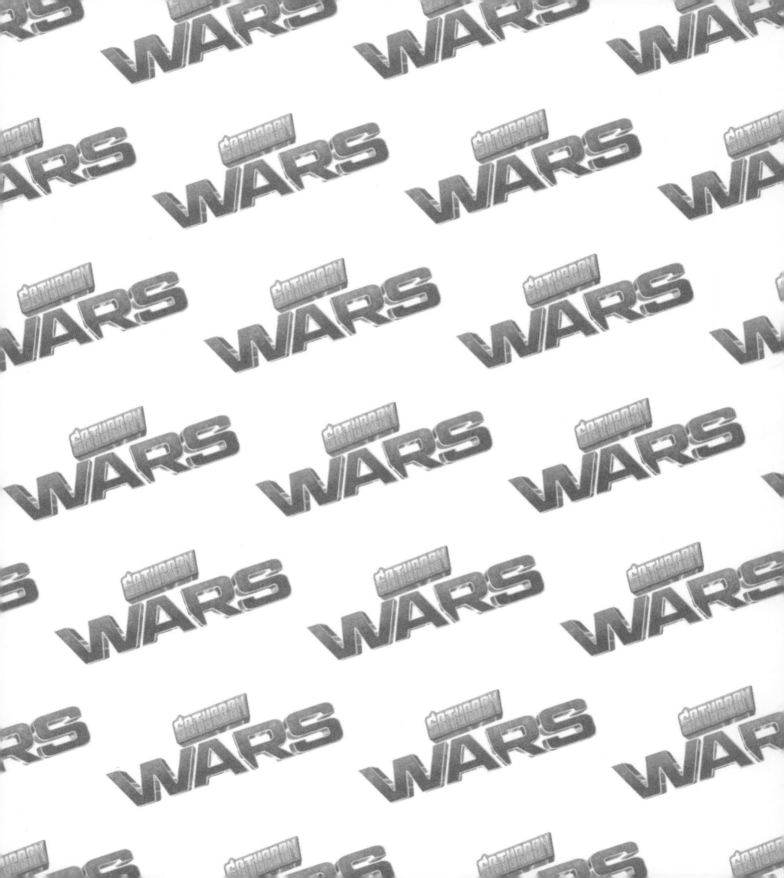

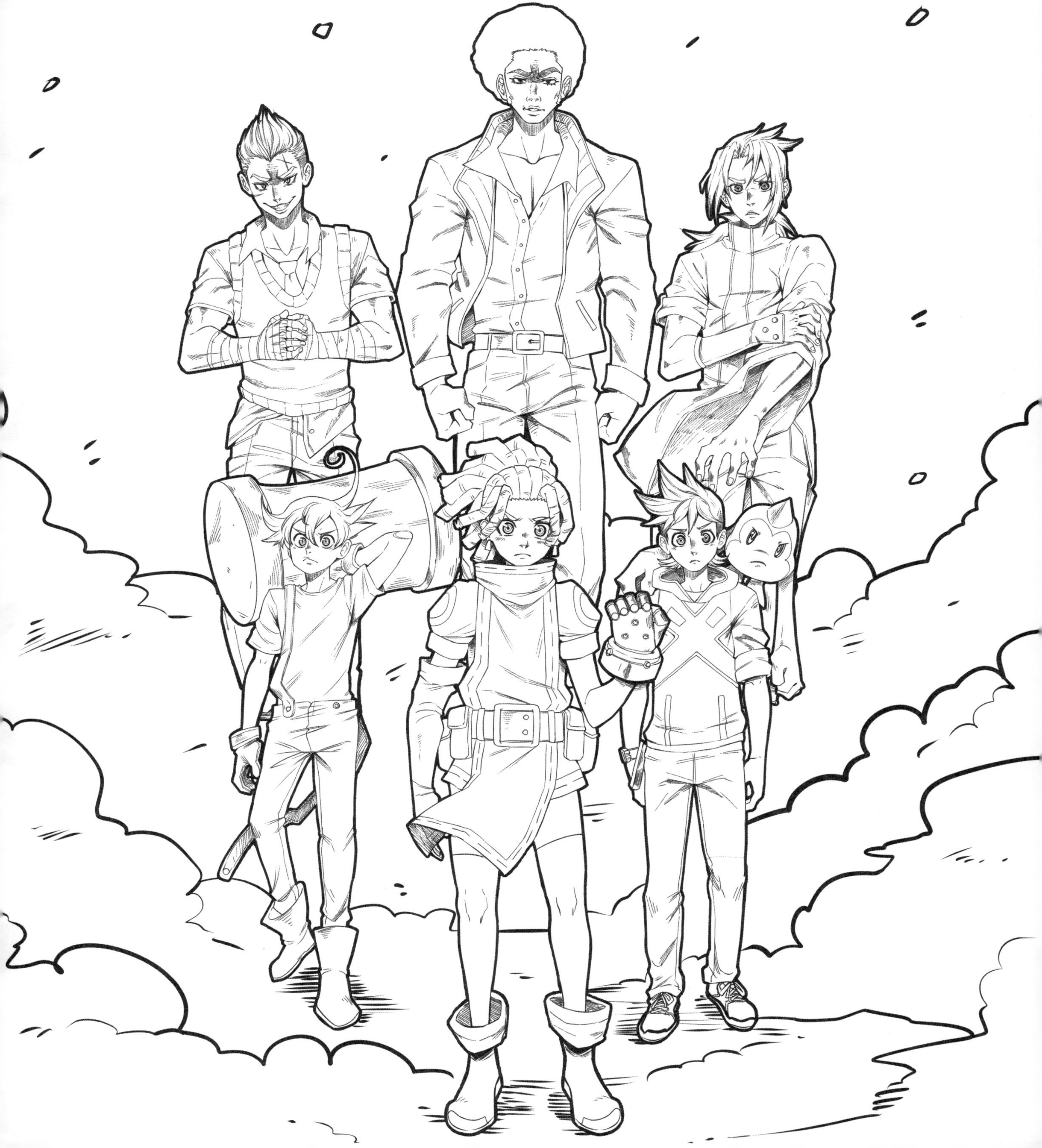

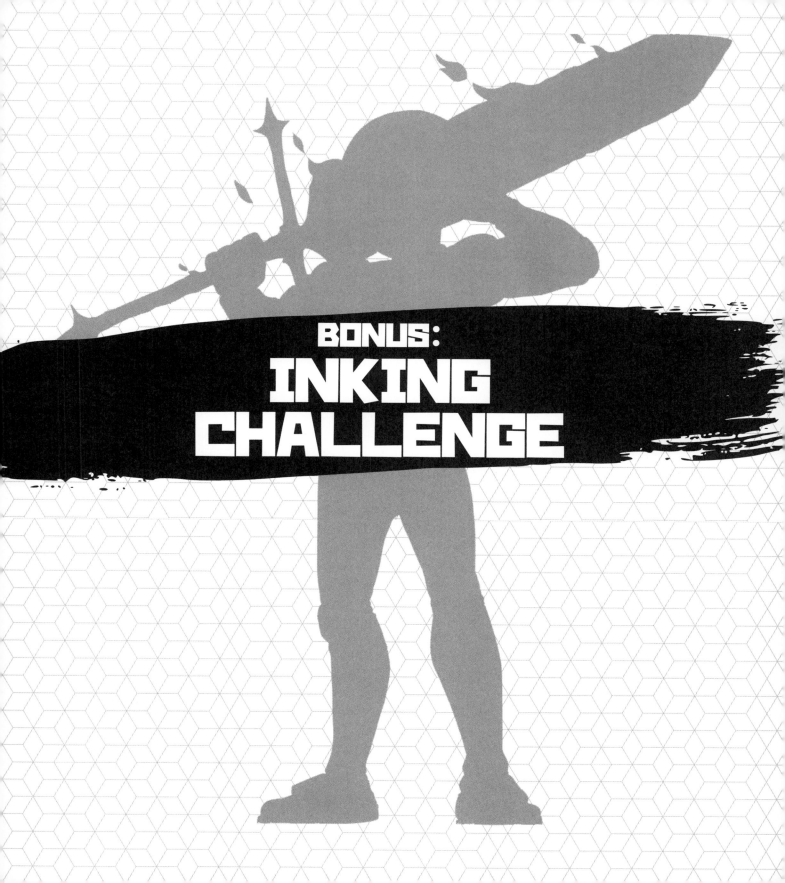

BONUS: INKING CHALLENGE

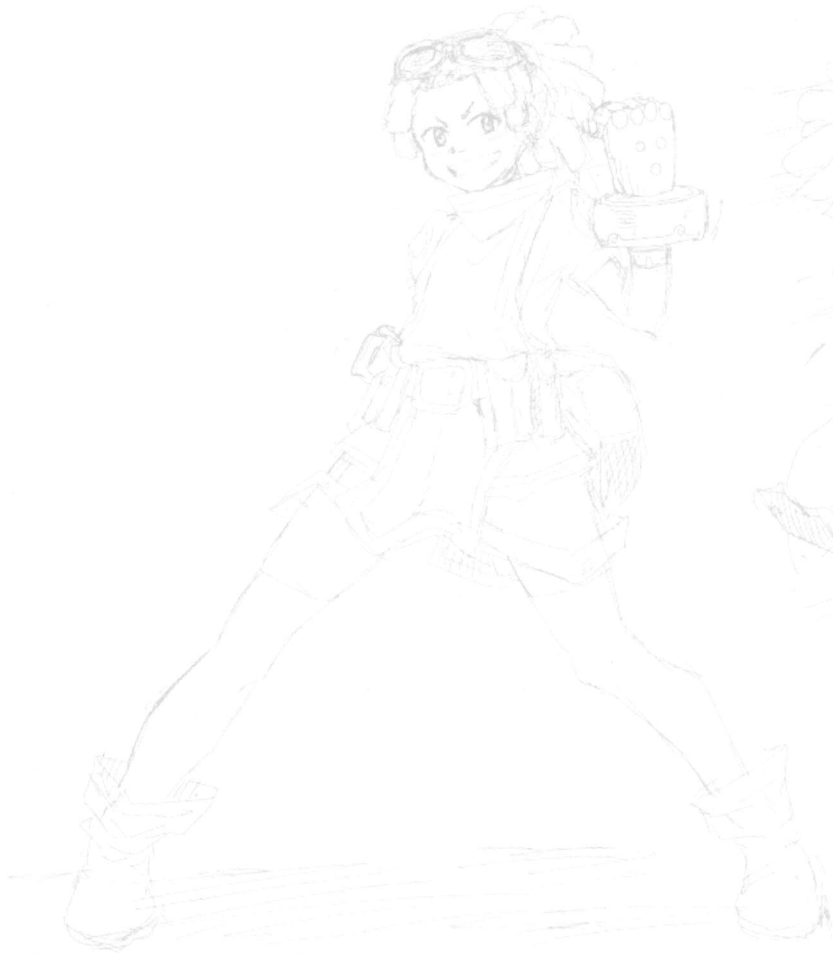

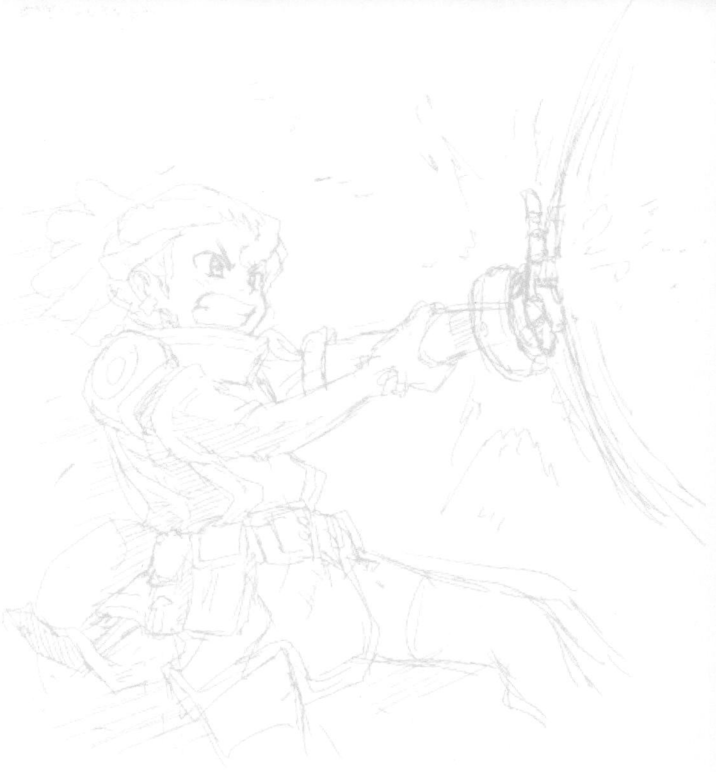

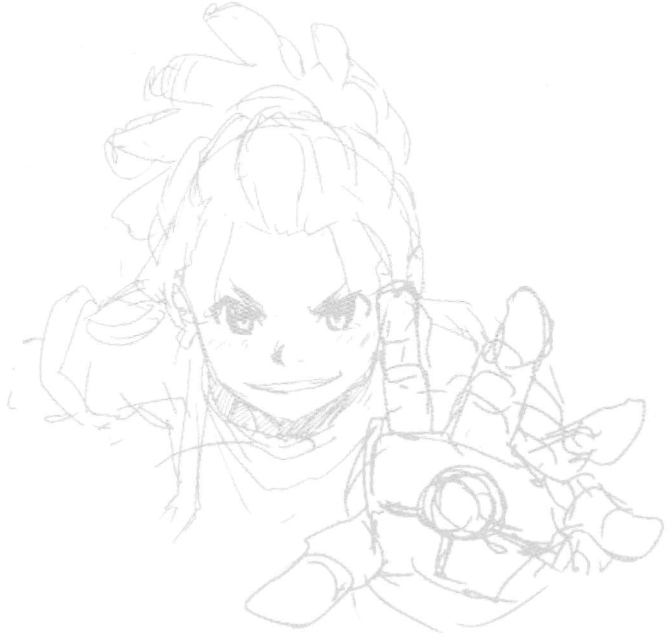

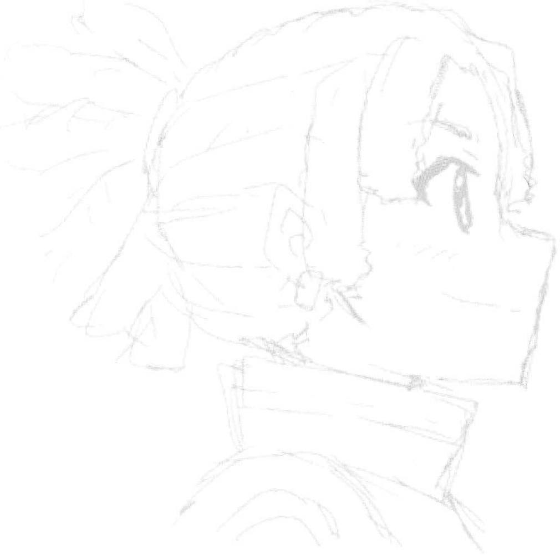

SATURDAY AM

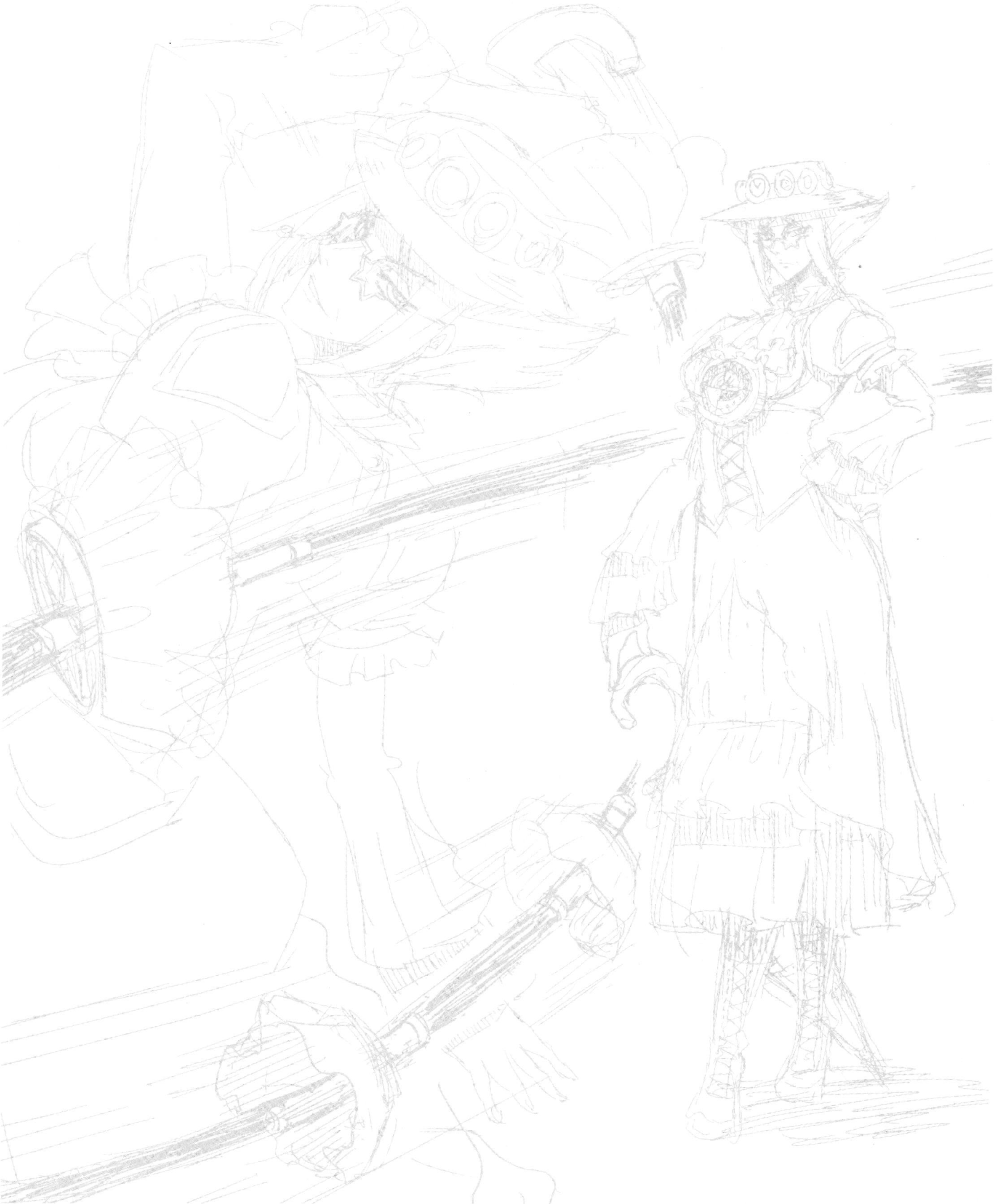

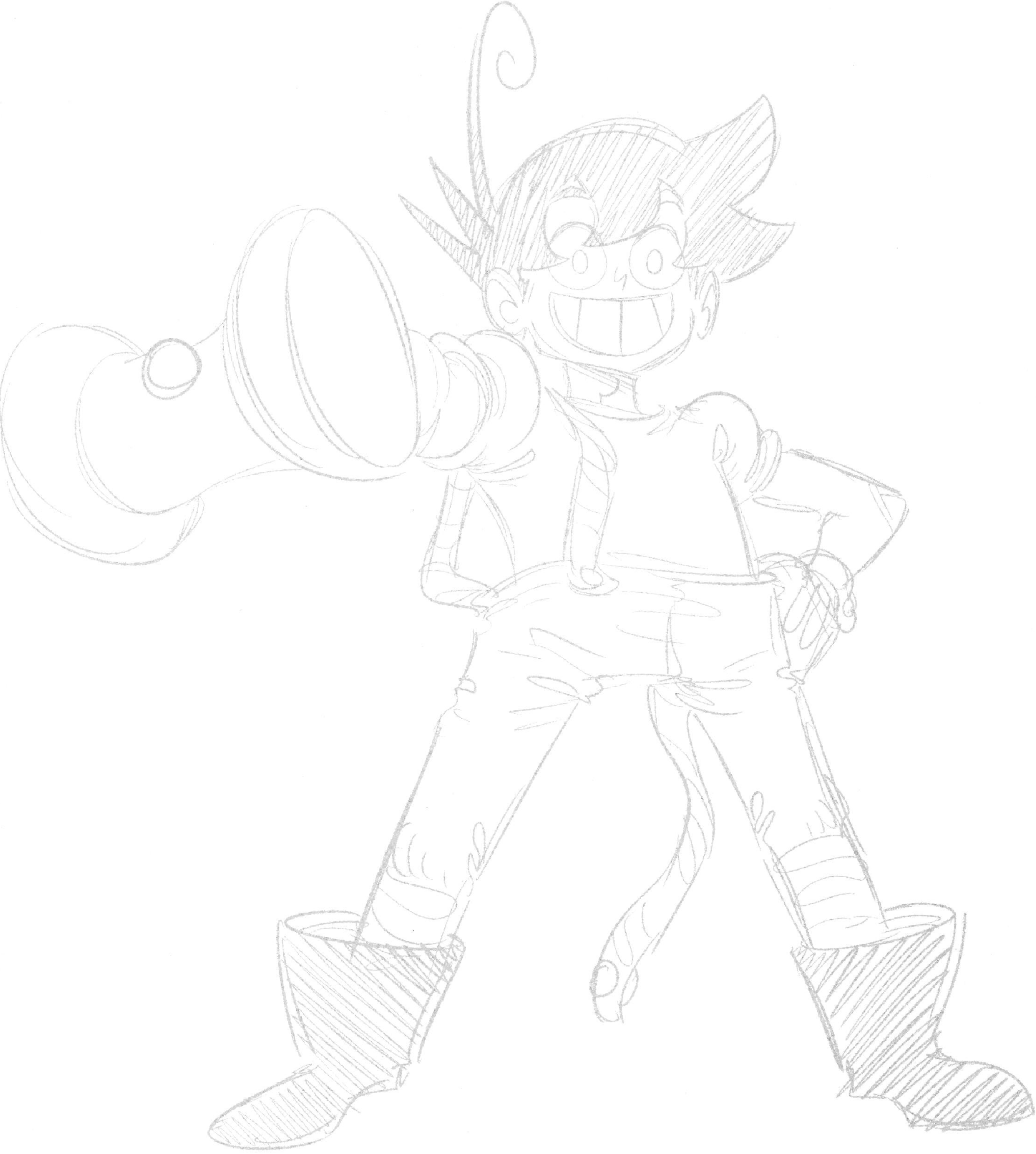

SATURDAY AM

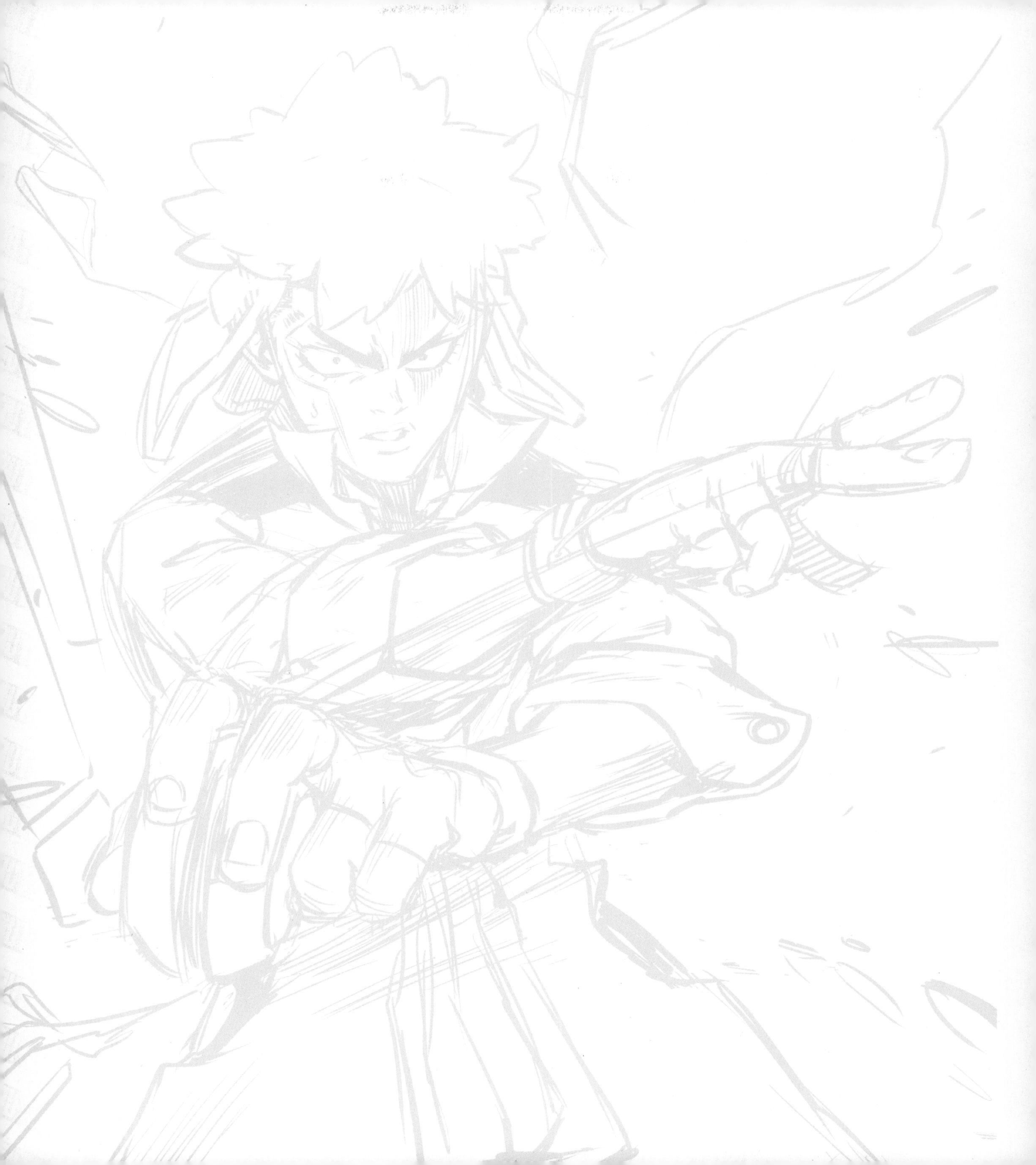

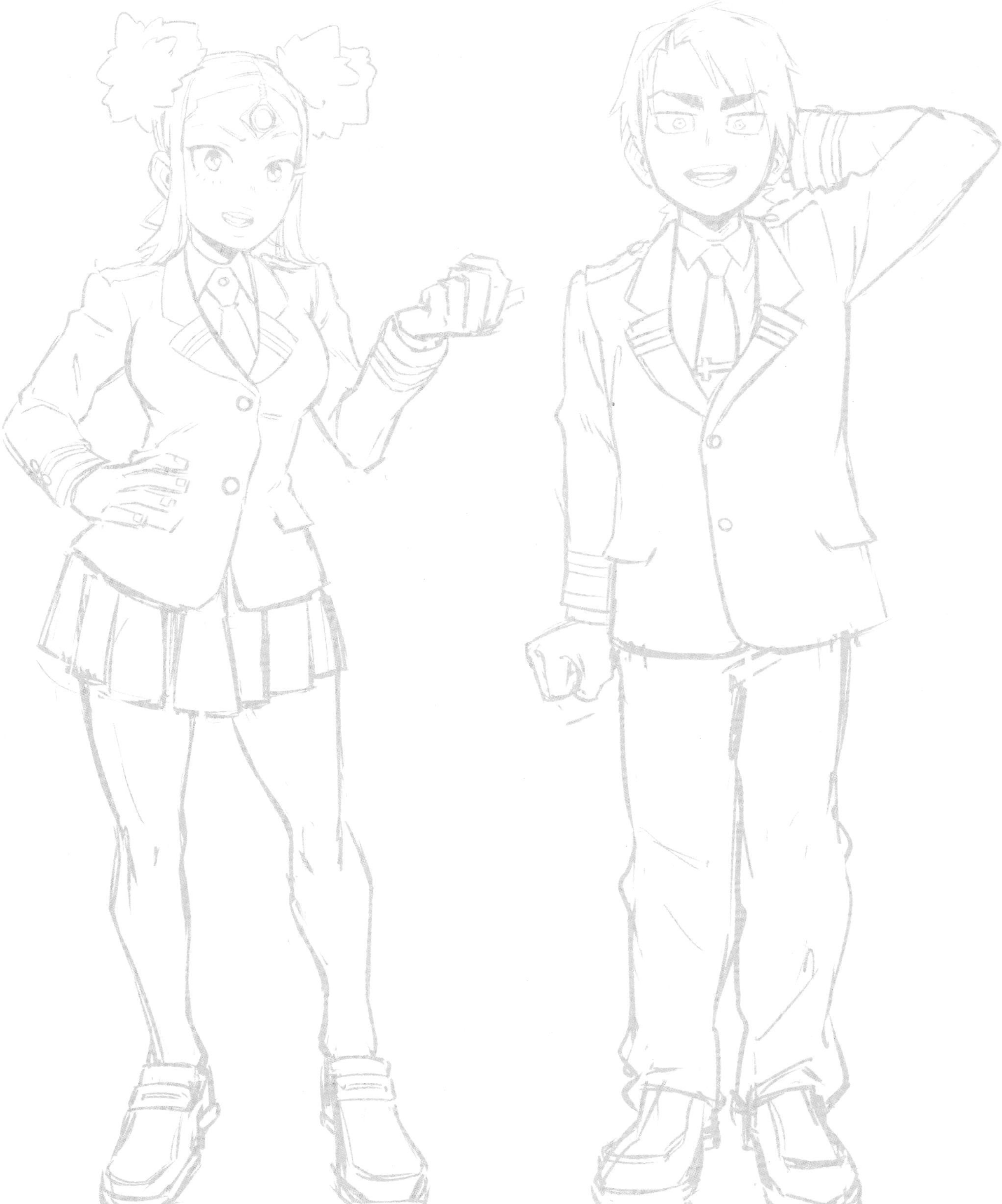

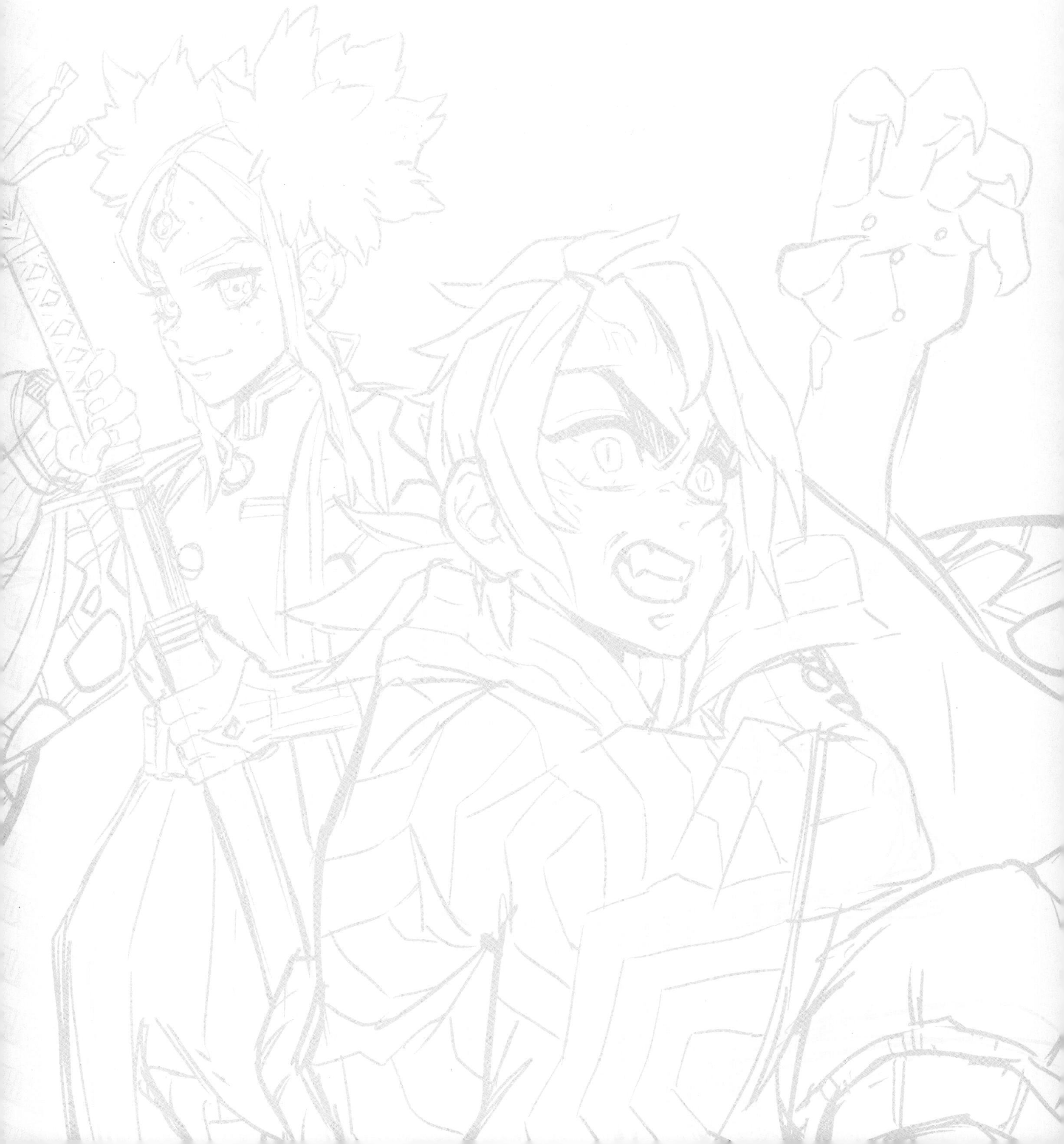

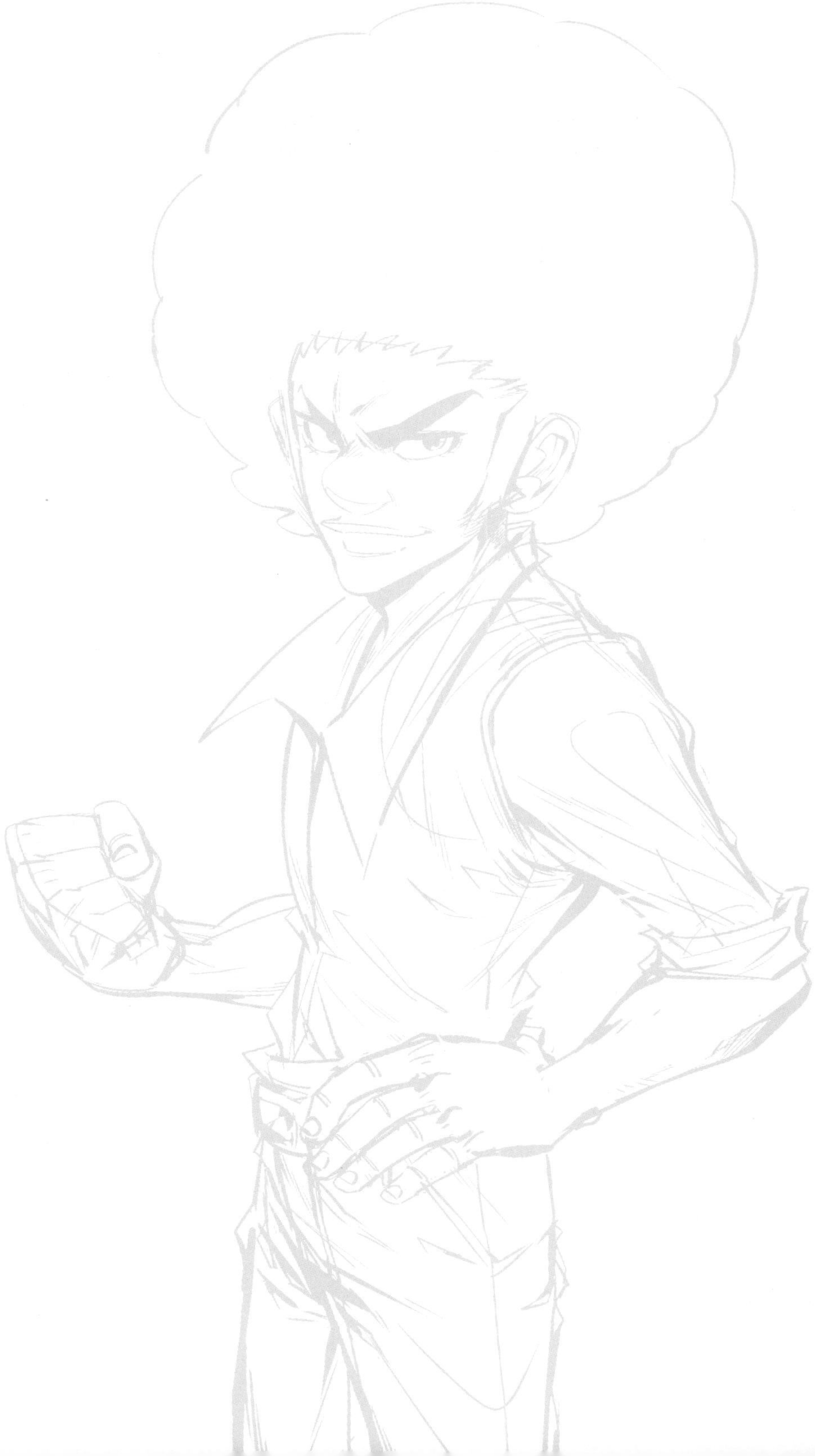

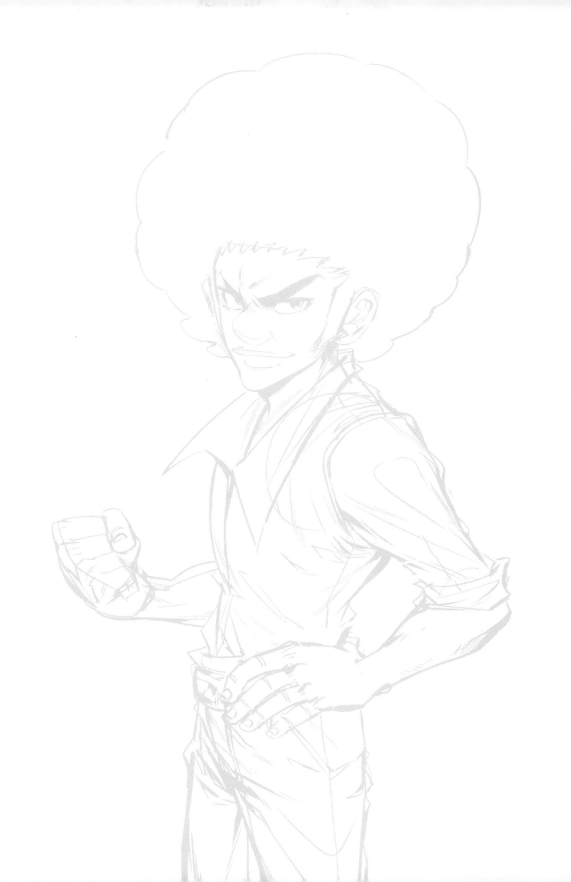

Quarto.com

© 2024 Quarto Publishing Group USA Inc.
Text and Illustrations © 2024 MyFutprint Entertainment

First published in 2024 by Rockport Publishers, an imprint of The Quarto Group,
100 Cummings Center, Suite 265-D, Beverly, MA 01915, USA.
T (978) 282-9590 F (978) 283-2742

Rockport Publishers titles are also available at discount for retail, wholesale, promotional, and bulk purchase. For details, contact the Special Sales Manager by email at specialsales@quarto.com or by mail at The Quarto Group, Attn: Special Sales Manager, 100 Cummings Center, Suite 265-D, Beverly, MA 01915, USA.

10 9 8 7 6 5 4 3 2 1

ISBN: 978-0-7603-8991-1

Design: Raymond Brown
Cover Image: The Creators and Arists at Saturday AM
Page Layout: Raymond Brown
Illustration: The Creators and Arists at Saturday AM

Printed in China